I0482841

TABLE OF CONTENTS

Social Media Body Language
How To Spot the Con Artists of Social Media
©Copyright 2013 by Dr. Harry Jay

DISCLAIMER AND TERMS OF USE AGREEMENT:

(Please Read This Before Using This Book)

This information is for educational and informational purposes only. The content is not intended to be a substitute for any professional advice, diagnosis, or treatment.

The authors and publisher of this book and the accompanying materials have used their best efforts in preparing this book.

The authors and publisher make no representation or warranties with respect to the accuracy, applicability, fitness, or completeness of the contents of this book. The information contained in this book is strictly for educational purposes. Therefore, if you wish to apply ideas contained in this book, you are taking full responsibility for your actions.

The authors and publisher disclaim any warranties (express or implied), merchantability, or fitness for any particular purpose. The author and publisher shall in no event be held liable to any party for any direct, indirect, punitive, special, incidental or other consequential damages arising directly or indirectly from any use of this material, which is provided "as is", and without warranties. As always, the advice of a competent legal, tax, accounting, medical or other professional should be sought where applicable.

The authors and publisher do not warrant the performance, effectiveness or applicability of any sites listed or linked to in this book. All links are for information purposes only and are not warranted for content, accuracy or any other implied or explicit purpose. No part of this may be copied, or changed in any format, or used in any way other than what is outlined within this course under any circumstances. Violators will be prosecuted.

This book is © Copyrighted by ePubWealth.com.

"No Crimes Beyond Forgiveness"

I am a felon, a thief of life
I take what I want, the devil be damned
I care not of the consequences of my lust
Am I any different than Uncle Sam?

To rationalize my sin is easy for
My life can't seem to get enough
It's not anything of yours that I pilfer
It's not any of what you call stuff

What I take I use and I use it well
I always give back more than I take
To have is to lose and to lose is to have
Remember this or you'll never forsake

All that is manna, you've not learned a thing
I take only knowledge from you
Call me a thief, a felon and more
But I now give more than I take back to you

Read my words; learn of my pain
Avoid all that I did wrong
I took only a jumble of words from you
Now I give them back as a song

Yes, I'm a criminal, a felon, a thief
I took what wasn't mine but for a purpose
Learn to forgive, learn to love but learn most of all
There are no crimes beyond forgiveness

Some readers might be confused by my title "Social Media Body Language". After all, social media sites and sites such as chat rooms and dating sites are mostly written content rather than a visual expression.

So what do I mean by "Social Media Body Language"? I will explain in just a moment…

In my books Body Language and Body Talk, I make the distinction that Body Language is the covert or involuntary physical expression of body gestures and posturing while Body Talk is the overt or purposeful use of body gestures and posturing.

Both are visual expressions.

In "Social Media Body Language," I am going to teach you how written content can be used to determine the exact same things that visual Body Language and Body Talk convey.

One is visual, the other is written but both can be analyzed to determine many things.

As a Senior Forensics Investigator with ForensicsNation.com and also as a behavioral science doctor, I am brought in to profile perpetrators of cyber crime.

I am the one that reviews transcripts of chat vroom logs, dating site profiles and social media dialogs and interaction to determine if criminal intent is present and then profile the criminal involved.

And you would be totally amazed at what I find.

Confessions of a Child Predator

An interview with a convicted child predator who caused the death of 5-teenagers

In my book, "Confessions of a Child Predator" I use the case files of two women – a mother and daughter – who were responsible for the deaths of five teenage boys.

I was brought in on the case because our investigative team was completely stumped. Nothing made sense about this case; it didn't follow any cyber-crime patterns or "modus operandi".

What I discovered quite quickly was that these women were posing as men and our investigators had been looking for men.

Men make up the majority of sexual predators but women make up the worst.

How did I discover that these were women and not men? I am going to show you how in this book.

But first, I need you to watch the ForensicsNation's Free Public Awareness Online Seminar to better understand just what the general public and business community is facing when it comes to cyber-crime.

Go to http://www.addmeinnow.com and sign up for the free online seminar. Please watch this before going any further in this book because I will be referring back to the contents of this seminar quite often.

I would also like to make you aware of another very valuable resource offered by one of my associates. He too, like me, is a forensics investigator and research scientist at Applied Mind Sciences, which is our company's mind research facility.

He offers a program that he teaches to law enforcement called "The Power of Trained Observation".

You can find these books by going online to the ePubWealth.com Library Catalog:
EPW Library Catalog Online
http://www.epubwealth.com/wp-content/uploads/2013/07/Leland-benton-private-turbo.pdf

EPW Library Catalog Download
http://www.filefactory.com/f/562ef3ea1a054f0a

This program was only offered to law enforcement but recently has been made available to the general public. This program teaches you how to see and hear everything and not miss a thing.

Learning to observe is very important. If you don't see danger and harm coming, what I am about to teach you would be worthless.

Okay, sit back and be prepared to be AMAZED. This is very interesting stuff and as in all of my mind science books I want to begin by teaching you some behavioral science about the human mind.

It is called "Laying a Proper Foundation" and this section is so very important because you will begin to see how the criminal mind function. You will also see why people do the things they do and why YOU do the things YOU do.

So let's get to the good stuff.

Forward – Laying A Proper Foundation

In all of my "Why" series of books, I will provide the following discourse on the Human Mind in order to lay a proper foundation to what I am about to teach.

The Mechanism of the Human Mind

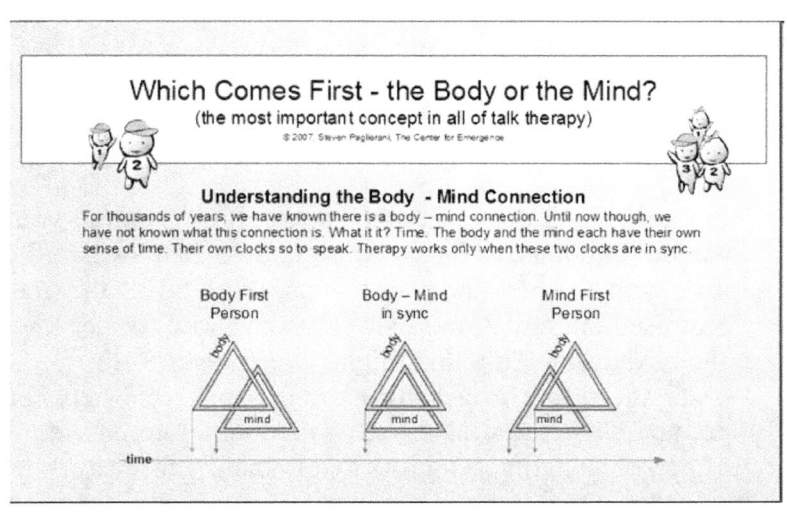

Which Comes First - the Body or the Mind?

(the most important concept in all of talk therapy)

© 2007. Steven Paglierani, The Center for Emergence

Understanding the Body - Mind Connection

For thousands of years, we have known there is a body – mind connection. Until now though, we have not known what this connection is. What it it? Time. The body and the mind each have their own sense of time. Their own clocks so to speak. Therapy works only when these two clocks are in sync.

| Body First Person | Body – Mind in sync | Mind First Person |

time

Prior to the fall of man into sin as described in the Garden of Eden, man's spirit was hooked to God's infinite spirit. There was no death because God's spirit is infinite. Man

11

is the only animal on earth that shares the eternality nature of God. The subject of eternal life has been a heated topic of man from the beginning of our existence.

In Greek mythology, there's a story about a mortal youth named Tithonus. Aurora, the goddess of dawn, fell in love with the boy and when Zeus, the king of the gods, promised to grant Aurora any gift she chose for her lover, she asked that Tithonus might live forever. But, in her haste she forgot to ask for eternal youth, so when Zeus granted her request, Tithonus was doomed to an eternity of perpetual aging as a grouchy old man... forever.

In the movie "Highlander," Angus McLeod was born in 1518 as an immortal being. He could not die and to me, the best part of the movie was the depiction of this immortal's agony here on earth as he watched everything he loved die forcing him to begin his life over and over again. He saw all of the ugliness, which man had caused over four centuries. He witnessed the Spanish Inquisition, Waterloo, the atrocities of the Third Reich, and more. He saw the slavery and bigotry of the eighteenth century, the slaughter of the Native American tribes after the Civil War. This man's life was a living Hell!

There is a very big difference between the ways our feeble minds picture eternal life versus God's idea of eternal life. Our understanding comes from Quantum Physics and is limited within the Time-Space Continuum.

Life is your spirit, but the soul of man has usurped the spirit's position and psychology is now forced to define "how" we live our lives based on the animating force of the soul instead of the spirit. As I said previously, the soul has usurped the spirit's place as our animating force. Let's discuss this now.

- ❖ **Body First Person** - When the body becomes our life, we live as animals.
- ❖ **Body-Mind In Sync** - When the soul becomes our life, we live as rebels and fugitives in a life of desires, emotions, and will (consuming entities). This is the position of mankind today!
- ❖ **Mind First Person** - But when we come to live our life in the mind/spirit and by the spirit, though we still use our soul's faculties just as we do our physical faculties, they are now the servants of the spirit.

If you live as a consuming entity, you will always lose. In other words, to get, you must give - you must sacrifice! Have you ever wondered why you have so many anxieties, phobias, worries and fears? The reality of this world is evil. So what is reality? I will tell you. This is reality:

"Life without war is impossible either in nature or in grace. The basis of physical, mental, moral and spiritual life is antagonism. Health is the balance between physical life and external nature, and it is maintained only by sufficient vitality on the inside against things on the outside. Everything outside my physical life is designed to put me to death. Things, which keep me going when I am alive, disintegrate me when I am dead. If I have enough fighting power, I produce the balance of health.

The same is true of mental life. If I want to maintain a vigorous mental life, I have to fight, and in that way the mental balance called thought is produced. Morally it is the same. Everything that does not partake of the nature of virtue is the enemy of virtue in me, and it depends on what moral caliber I have whether I overcome and produce virtue (GOOD CHARACTER). Immediately I fight, I am moral in that particular. No man is virtuous because he cannot help it; virtue (character) is acquired.

- ❖ Psychology only studies the observable aspects of the mind and discounts the unseen or intangible aspects of the human mind.
- ❖ Behavioral science attempts to study the intangible aspects of the human mind…why you do the things you do and more importantly why you don't do what you should do.
- ❖ There is no such thing as commercial psychology versus personal psychology. The mind uses the same mechanism to evaluate all types of relationships.
- ❖ Everything we do revolves around relationships. We relate to our environment, our friends, family, co-workers, other people and even our pets. We are social animals.

The Mechanism of the Human Mind

Belief Systems + Thought + Delight = Action/Behavior/Conduct

Conscious Mind

5-senses:

Sight
Hearing
Taste
Touch
Smell
ESP (women only)

Subconscious Mind

Intellect:
Experiential
Empirical

DEW:
Desires, Emotions and Will

The Human Psyche Differences Between Genders

The female psyche operates on emotional, spiritual, physical and intellectual planes
The male psyche operates only on the intellectual and physical planes.

Here is an exercise you might find weird but it demonstrates the power of the human mind.

Fi yuo cna raed tihs, yuo hvae a sgtrane mnid too. Cna yuo raed tihs? Olny 55 plepoe out of 100 can. I cdnuolt blveiee taht I cluod aulaclty uesdnatnrd waht I was rdanieg. The phaonmneal pweor of the hmuan mnid, aoccdrnig to a rscheearch at Cmabrigde Uinervtisy, it dseno't mtaetr in waht oerdr the ltteres in a wrod are, the olny iproamtnt tihng is taht the frsit

and lsat ltteer be in the rghit pclae. The rset can be a taotl mses and you can sitll raed it whotuit a pboerlm. Tihs is bcuseae the huamn mnid deos not raed ervey lteter by istlef, but the wrod as a wlohe. Azanmig huh? Yaeh and I awlyas tghuhot slpeling was ipmorantt!

You might have found it somewhat unusual that you could probably read the jumbled mess above. Actually over half the people that see this exercise can decipher the words at the same speed of reading as if the words were not jumbled.

It is important to note that the human mind thinks in packages…concepts rather than individual ideas.

Your eyes see each letter but the mind looks at the whole word instead. As you read, the mind looks at the first and last letter only. Remember this; the mind sees the beginning and end. We will talk about this later…

If you were to listen to an orchestra, your ear listens to every note from every instrument but a trained ear can actually pick out individual instruments from the whole sound as the mind hears the whole symphony.

How does this apply to you?

Learning to observe means going beyond the mind's natural ability to only read the first and last letters of a word!

It is training the mind to see all the letters, not just the eye but the mind!

Truisms About the Human Mind

❖ Pain vs. Pleasure – people are more motivated to avoid pain than seek pleasure.
❖ A person that is suffering depression will seek relief (notice I didn't say cure) before they seek happiness.
❖ The human mind cannot tell the difference between fantasy and reality.
❖ The human mind gravitates to the desires, emotions and will of its psyche. People crave entertainment so fantasy dominates their existences.
❖ The human mind is easily distracted! You can either be the cause of these distractions or other stimuli will be the cause but rest assured people WILL BE distracted because the human mind is gullible.

The human mind responds quickly to these three forms of stimuli

❖ Sex
❖ Humor
❖ FEAR

But the greatest of them all is FEAR!

BTW – on the positive side we have faith, hope, love, but the greatest of these *is* LOVE.

Fear usually takes the form of what is called "Scarcity Thought"

You are afraid that someone will have what you feel belongs to you or that others will have more "stuff" than you.

❖ The subconscious mind is often referred to as the "heart," and is the control mechanism the body uses to store our beliefs.

❖ **These beliefs are stored as pictures in our "hearts" and create frequencies in our bodies.**

❖ We know that the optimum human frequency is a little below 7.83 hertz. To drop below this frequency brings on the onslaught of disease. To rise above it a person demonstrates psychic abilities.

❖ Harmful beliefs that cause unhealthy frequencies are the source of almost all problems - physical, mental, emotional.

❖ The subconscious mind creates a belief system, which we call "pictures of the heart."

❖ These pictures involve either visions, or dreams/fantasies.

❖ Science has discovered that the subconscious mind cannot distinguish between fantasy and reality.

*The subject of all dreams is the dreamer.
*Dreams are born in our desires, emotions and will.
*Dreamers believe in a belief system, which is fantasy.

*A life lived within a fantasy creates a feeling of self-centeredness, hopelessness and despair. In dreams everything is perfect.

*The subject of a vision is not the visionary but the world.

*Visions are born in the intellect.

*Visions are pictures of the future that have already been experienced in the heart of those who give it birth.

*Visionaries sacrifice themselves for the good of mankind.

*Visions have a moral quality that transcends the self-centered nature of dreams.

*By its very nature a vision launches a mission, a "cause-that-inspires."

*Visions create a sense of belonging.

❖ We act upon visions and/or dreams, using thought.

❖ Thought employs the intellect, in the case of visions, or the desires, emotions and the will, in the case of dreams.

❖ Intellectual thought relies on wisdom; emotional thought relies on the pursuit of pleasure, comfort and delight.

❖ Dreamers live within a facade; they create a false sense of worth using imaginary situations.

❖ Visionaries live within reality; they create change, within a framework of restraint, and intellectual thought.

❖ The world is made up of OPPOSITES, which is usually the corrupted version of the original. We have good and evil. We have love and lust!

❖ EVERYTHING YOU DO IS BECAUSE OF LOVE OR LUST. Learn to love because there are no crimes beyond forgiveness.

*Love is born in the intellect; lust is born in the DEW!
*Love is vision; lust is fantasy.
*Love restrains & sacrifices; lust is selfish
*Love is being one with someone or something
*Lust is being with someone or something.
*Visionaries love; dreamers lust!
*Visionaries do what is required; dreamers just do their best!

WHEN THERE IS NO HOPE OF LOVE DO WE ABANDON OURSELVES TO LUST?

Yes we do!

Pictures of the heart are your belief system.

❖ We animate these pictures into either fantasies, or visions.
❖ People do not appear to see the difference between the matter part of an organism and the life part, which animates it.
❖ We seem to think that the organism itself is life. In other words, it is not our outward appearance that is our life, but our inward existence.
❖ Life is what goes into the body. Death is what comes out.
❖ A person who lies is not a liar because he tells a lie. The lie is the manifested behavior of some

20

subconscious belief system. The lie only demonstrates that the person is a liar…it is the effect.

❖ Except for love, the power of words inspired by a vision or fantasy is the most potent human force.

"Do you want to have or do you want to be?"

*For a dreamer: "Seeing is believing!"
*But they only see imaginary things that are not real!!
*This is why "The Secret" is WRONG!
*Say it and claim it is WRONG!
*Blab it and grab it IS WRONG!
*See it and be it IS WRONG!
Dreamers practice companionship – To be with someone or something!

VERY IMPORTANT:

1. Dreamers covet the object of their temptation, BUT they covet the temptation more so than the object itself because the temptation is the idol of their fantasy.
2. If there is a conflict between the conscious and subconscious mind, the subconscious mind always wins…ALWAYS!
3. All reaction occurs in the conscious mind; all interaction occurs in the subconscious mind. Fear is a "REACTION" to losing control.

For a visionary: "Believing is seeing!"

There are no SECRETS; there are only challenges to be conquered!

THIS IS NOT A SECRET: Putting a photo of a Ferrari on your refrigerator and seeing yourself driving it by employing the so-called law of attraction is pure BUPKES!!! Why? Because this is all occurring in the conscious mind and beliefs reside in the subconscious mind. How do you transfer something from the conscious mind to the subconscious mind and make it a belief system?

A Ferrari is the object of your temptation but what you covet most is the temptation of owning a Ferrari because the temptation is the idol of your fantasy.

It is all about ATTENTION & ACCEPTANCE!!!!! I have a $100 bill in my hand and I am willing to give it to you. But if you don't ACCEPT it then it is still in my hand. BELIEF SYSTEMS ARE CREATED BY ATTENTION & ACCEPTANCE!

John 1:12 But as many as received him, to them gave he **the right** to become children of God, *even* to them that believe on his name

Human things must be known to be loved; but divine things must be loved to be known.

BELIEVING IS SEEING!

Let's talk about goals...which of the following goals are good goals?

- ❖ To want to get married and have a wonderful, happy, loving marriage?
- ❖ To want to have children who are happy, successful, and loving?
- ❖ To have a successful, fulfilling and rewarding career?
- ❖ Is it a good goal to want to have fun, bonded, loving, and meaningful relationships with other people?

Which of the listed goals are good goals? None of them!

You should never have anything for a goal that is not 100% under your control, AND each and every goal should be <u>motivated by love</u>.

Almost all goals that we have in our life are wrong.

Everything that we do, we do because of a goal we have.

When we get up in the morning, it's because of some goal that we have; we are hungry for breakfast, or we need to go to work.

If we go to the grocery store, it's because of some goal we have. If we are kind to people, it's because of some goal that we have.

Now we don't always know what they are, because a lot of these are subconscious goals.

The goals we have are the reasons for everything we do. But, do all of your goals involve only YOU?

Of course not!

And when the other person, or persons, in your goal do not perform, or act the way you want them to, then we become anxious and stressed.

When our goals get blocked, it creates anger, anxiety, and frustration. If we only have good goals, we will not experience anger or anxiety.

That's how you know, if you are living a wrongful goal. If the result is anger and frustration because your control was blocked and blocking your goal, then you had a wrongful goal. It may have been a fine and noble desire, but a wrongful goal.

Filters
We live in a society of consumerism and entertainment. In my previous books I have spoken reams about this subject. Instant gratification is paramount and today's technology delivers information and other stimuli in bucketfuls to the human mind. We have already spoken about filters that the human mind employs to weed out what it determines to be irrelevant. This "irrelevancy" is different in every individual and many times is programmed into our minds subconsciously or without us knowing it. We have also spoken about the causes of these various filters such as environment, maturity, upbringing, culture, etc.

The one essential common element of all filters is that they are all ATTENTION diverters. We have spoken about attention earlier; what is very interesting is that filters are generally viewed as bad when some are really very good.

I had a friend, who lives in Chicago, fall on hard times and needed assistance. When I got to him he was living in a cheap hotel and had a room so small when you put the key in the door you broke the *window (I slay me)*. His room was about 50 feet from the Loop (the overhead train that circles around Chicago). The noise was deafening when the train went by, and it went by often, but my friend had filtered it out. Amazing, but when you thing about it, my friend really does hear the train but yet he pays no attention to it, so in actuality, it is like he doesn't hear it at all! So filters divert attention, and take away our focus; so let's talk about focus.

The Incredible Power of Focus
One of the more important points I have made has been the idea that you really do create your own life and your own reality. I know this idea has become a kind of personal growth cliché that many of us have heard over and over for years. Many people, after continuing to experience the same old ups and downs and personal dramas over many years, get to the point where they dismiss this idea as charming but useless -- or just plain wrong. "If I'm creating this, then I'm certainly not doing it on purpose," they say. "It sure seems like this is HAPPENING to me, rather than that I'm creating it." They just assume that it's all BS because "this and this and this and this are going on for me, and I have no control over it, and anyone who thinks I'm creating this doesn't understand what I'm going through." Essentially, they are resigning themselves to becoming a victim of circumstances.

We live in a universe of infinite complexity and many forces -- way too many to keep track of -- operate on us. Yes, it is true that we are NOT in control of everything that happens, because we are not in control of most of those infinite other parts of the universe. In fact, the only thing you have total and complete control over is...YOUR OWN MIND. That is, if you learn how to exercise it.

Luckily, this one thing -- your mind -- that you do have control over gives you tremendous power. By exercising control over your mind, you can get the rest of those infinite other parts of the universe to begin to march in formation.

The person who says, "If I'm creating this, it certainly isn't on purpose," is right. They are not creating what is happening to them "on purpose." Who would purposely create failure, or bad relationships, or any other kind of suffering? You can only do something that is not good for you that is harmful to you, if you do it subconsciously. This means if you are creating something you don't want, you must be doing so subconsciously.

Your mind is running on automatic pilot, based on "software" (subconscious programming) installed when you were too young to know any better, by parents, teachers, friends, the media, and other experiences and influences. The key is to become more conscious, more aware...to get yourself off automatic pilot. Once you do this, you stop creating all the dramas and other garbage you don't want in your life.

How do you do this? One way is by remembering and using a very important piece of wisdom. What is this important piece of wisdom? I'm glad you asked.

It's the fact that whatever you focus on manifests as reality in your life.

You are always focusing on something, whether you are aware of it or not. If I spent some time with you, and heard your history, I could tell you what you are focusing on. How? By looking at the results you are getting in your life. The results you get are always the result of your focus.

The problem is this focus is usually not conscious focus; it's automatic or subconscious focus. We subconsciously focus on something we don't want, and then when we get it we feel like a victim and don't even stop to think that we created it in the first place. And what is more, we don't realize we could choose to create something completely different if we could only get out of the cycle of subconsciously focusing on something other than what we want.

If you have a significant negative emotional experience (say, for instance, a relationship in which you are abused or mistreated in some way), a part of you is going to say: "Okay, I get it. There are people out there who can and will hurt me. Relationships can be dangerous and painful. I have to watch out for these people [or sometimes, relationships in general] and avoid them." Unfortunately, to watch out for them and avoid them, you have to focus your mind on "people who could hurt me," or "bad relationships," and that focus draws more of what you don't want to you...AND...actually makes these things you don't want (at least initially) attractive to you, so when they appear in your life you are drawn to them. This is why many people keep having one relationship after another with the same person, but in different bodies. This, of course, applies to everything, not just relationships. I'm just using relationships as an example.

Focusing on what you do not want, ironically, makes it happen. Focusing on not being poor makes you poor. Focusing on not making mistakes causes you to make mistakes. Focusing on not having a bad relationship creates bad relationships. Focusing on not being depressed makes you depressed. Focusing on not smoking makes you want to smoke. And so on. I think you get the idea. The mind will create what you focus on both GOOD and BAD!!!

The truth is your mind cannot tell the difference between something you think about or focus on that you DO want, and something you think about or focus on but Do NOT want. The mind is a goal-seeking mechanism, and an extremely effective one at that. Already, all the time, it is elegantly and precisely creating exactly what you focus on. You are already a World Champion Expert at creating whatever you focus on. You couldn't get any better at it, and you don't need to get any better at it.

When you focus on anything, your mind says: "Okay, we can do that," and starts figuring out how to do it. It doesn't ask whether you're focusing on it because you want it or because you do not want it. It ALWAYS assumes you want what you focus on and then it goes and makes it happen. The more frequent and the more intense the focus, the faster and more completely you will create what you have focused on, which is why intense negative experiences create intense focus on what you do not want, and tend to make you re-create what you don't want, over and over.

Most of the time, for most people, all the focusing and thinking is going by at warp speed, on automatic, without much, if any, conscious intention. Your job is to learn how to direct this power by consciously directing your focus to the outcomes you want. Once you do, everything changes. This does, however, take some work, because at first you have to swim upstream against the current of your old, unconscious habits, and the current can be swift and strong. Trained observation actually teaches you to focus on what you want.

First, you have to discover all the things you focus on that you do not want, and I'm willing to bet there are quite a few -- way more than you think. To the degree you're getting what you don't want, you are focusing, albeit subconsciously, on what you don't want.

Spend some time over the next few weeks making a list of all the things you do NOT want as you notice yourself thinking about them.

Second, you have to get very clear about what you DO want. Then, you have to examine each of the things you want and be sure they are not just something you do NOT want in disguise. For instance, saying "I want a relationship where I am treated well" would not even be an issue if you had not had relationships where you were not treated well, and even in making this seemingly positive statement you are focusing on not wanting to be mistreated. Saying "I want a reliable car" wouldn't even come up if you weren't focusing on the fact that you don't want a car that breaks down and needs a lot of repairs.

After you've sorted out the things you habitually focus on that you do not want, and know what you do want, you have to begin to notice each time you think about an

29

outcome you do not want, and consciously change your thinking, right in that moment, so you are instead focusing on what you do want.

Remember, you do NOT have to avoid things to be happy and get what you want. The urge to avoid something is a result of having had a negative emotional experience regarding that thing, and trying to avoid things requires you to focus on them, which tells your brain to create them. Not good.

You will be surprised how often you are thinking about what you do not want, how difficult it is to catch yourself doing it every time, and -- most of all – how difficult it is to switch your thinking to what you DO want. There is a strong momentum to keep thinking about that thing you want to avoid. As I said, the current is strong and swift, especially at first.

The solution? Practice, practice, practice. Persistence, persistence, persistence!!!

It's a very good idea to write down what you want, very specifically, so that your Fairy Godmother, were she to read it, would know exactly what to give you without any additional explanation.

Then, read what you have written to yourself, preferably out loud, several times a day, while seeing yourself, in your mind, already having what you want.

Believing is seeing and not the other way around as the world teaches you!

The more emotion you can bring to it, the better. Then, take whatever action is available to begin moving toward what you want. A good time to do this reading and visualizing is when you first wake up and before you go to bed.

I know this is work. Do it anyway. There is a price for everything, and this is the price you must pay to get what you want. Be prepared to pay it. It will be worth it, I promise. And be prepared to pay for a while before you get results. Stick with it.

Another way to change your focus is to ask questions. As an example, I'll ask you one right now. What did you have for breakfast this morning? To answer this question (even to just internally process the question), you had to shift your focus from whatever your mind was focused on (hopefully, to what I am teaching) to today's breakfast.

This means that to change your focus, all you have to do is...ask yourself a question!

It also means you better be careful what questions you ask yourself. Good questions include "How can I get X?" "How can I do X?" "How can I be X?" By asking these kinds of questions, you get your mind to focus on what you want to have, do, or be. Then, your mind takes over and answers the question...solves the problem...and creates what you want. You just have to provide the focus, take whatever action presents itself, and be persistent (some things take time).

I would do away with questions like "What's wrong with me?" or "Why can't I find someone to love me?" and so on. Your mind will find an answer to any question you give it, including these disempowering questions.

Learn to say "How can I...?" when you don't know what to do, instead of "I can't," and (if you are persistent in asking) you will receive the answer, every time. Learn to

31

be conscious in what you focus on and your whole life will change.

This all may seem very utopian to you, or overly simplistic, or like a lot of work. I assure you it is not utopian (it's the way all successful people think), it IS simple, but not simplistic, and yes, it is work, at first. The great Napoleon Hill, who spent over 60 years studying the most effective and most successful people of the 20th century, concluded that -- without exception -- "whatever the mind can conceive and believe, it can achieve." He at first suspected there had to be exceptions, but toward the end of his life he said he had to admit he had not found ANY.

Let's go over that again: "Whatever the mind can conceive and believe it can achieve."

It will take some time to learn how to consciously focus your mind. It will require some effort. You will fail many times, and it will seem difficult. But at a certain point you will "get it" and at that point it will become as automatic as the unconscious focusing you have been doing. When that happens, a whole new universe of power will open to you.

More on Focusing

"And be not conformed to this age, but be transformed by the renewing of your mind, in order to prove by you what is the good and pleasing and perfect will of God."

The one thing in your life you can command is your own mind. Whatever negative people and situations you face, you can always choose a positive attitude. But doing so requires a firm, strong commitment.

Helpful: Begin by writing a self-convincing creed – I believe I can direct and control my emotions, intellect and habits with the intention of developing a positive mental attitude. Post it where you'll see it when you get up in the morning. Read it during the day, and say it aloud. Speaking an intention reinforces it. Choose a "self-motivator" – a meaningful phrase tailored to help you reach your positive thinking goals. Examples:

- Counter discouragement with the phrase "Every problem contains the seed of its own solution."

- Fight procrastination with "Do it now."

Keep your self-motivators nearby – in your pocket or on your desk – and repeat them throughout the day to instill these important new values.

Develop A Life Plan. Setting short and long-term goals each day creates a road map for your life. But only set GOOD goals!!! What is a good goal? One where you are 100% in control and one that is founded in love! A goal of raising good, healthy and prosperous children is a bad goal because you are not in control of what your kids choose. See the important difference? The goal is noble but it is not a good goal.

You identify where you're going, focus your mind on getting there and avoid many wrong turns.

Helpful: Use the D-E-S-I-R-E formula as a goal-setting guideline…

- **D**etermine what you want. Be exact, and express the goal positively. Say what you want to be or do rather than what you don't want.

- Evaluate what you'll give in return. How much work will you do to turn your plan into action?

- Set a date for your goal. Be realistic, allowing enough time without postponing it too long.

- Identify a step by step plan. Devise immediate, small steps to get started.

- Repeat your plan in writing.

- Each and every day, morning and evening, read your plan aloud as you picture yourself already having achieved your goals.

Writing out your daily goals helps maintain your motivation. Keep them in your pocket or purse to read frequently throughout the day.

The Power of Visualization
Because visual images reach into our deepest mental levels, I have found pictures to be profound motivational tools. Why? Remember the mind holds everything as pictures!

Helpful: Make a list of personal qualities you want to develop...write down the names of people with whom you would like to have better relationships. Now clip pictures from magazines and newspapers that symbolize your goals.

Example: If generosity is your chosen quality, you could use a photo of someone with an outstretched hand.

Put the pictures where you'll see them everyday...and believe that you will get what you have visualized. You may also create your own "mental pictures" to defeat negative thoughts, such as dwelling on past reversals.

Maintain A Positive Focus. Giving yourself positive experiences actually reinforces your positive attitude. Examples…

- Treat your five senses every day. Listen to your favorite music, taste a food you love, enjoy a beautiful view, etc.

- Cultivate a sense of humor. Laughter relaxes tension, and seeing the funny side of things helps you take yourself less seriously.

- Smile when you feel like frowning. Smile at yourself in the mirror. If this makes you laugh at yourself, the smile will be that much more real.

Now realize the optimistic face you show the world creates positive thoughts about you in everyone you meet.

How to Train Your Subconscious Mind
Did you know that often the difference between success and failure is the ability to train your mind to focus on achieving your goals and not focus on problems? It's been proven by researchers and by some of the most successful people in the world.

Getting your mind to focus and concentrate on success - so that it finds solutions instead of focusing on the problems is usually the difference between success and failure. But how do you do this?

I'm about to show you how. I'll outline the importance of training your mind, how to start directing your subconscious mind, and how to keep your mind focused so that you constantly achieve your goals and live the life you want. Disciplining your mind so that it is focused on your goals is crucial to your success. If your mind is not trained to focus on and achieve your goals then you really have little chance of success. Your conscious mind is a direct link to your subconscious mind.

So if your mind is focused on your goals and is trained to achieve those goals then your subconscious mind will also be focused on those goals and will attract the situations and opportunities for you to achieve the success you want. It's really that simple.

The minute you get distracted for a prolonged period - you lose sight of your objective and fail to accomplish those goals. In order for to enjoy success - the mind has to be regularly focused on your goals - you can't stay focused for short bursts and expect to get results.

Think of it this way, your riding in a car driven by your personal driver and every time your driver asks you where you want to go you simply say: "I don't know. Wherever you want to go is fine with me." Then when your driver takes you to the place of his choice you complain and say: "I don't want to be here, take me somewhere else." And again you say you don't know where you want to go.

Can you see the confusion you would create? Can you see how you would never get to where you want to go because you haven't trained your driver to automatically take you where you want to go? You haven't given him the proper instructions.

Your mind and subconscious mind work the same way. If you don't train your mind to focus on your goals then your subconscious mind cannot create the situations that will help you achieve those goals. When you keep changing your mind, when you are not clear on what you want - your subconscious gets confused - and you end up exactly where you don't want to be.

Let's go back to the example of your personal driver. Wouldn't it be a lot easier and more comfortable if you told your driver where you wanted to go - or even better - your driver knew where you wanted to go ahead of time? But that will only happen when you train your driver by repeatedly telling him where you want to go on a regular basis.

Your subconscious mind is your driver. Your subconscious gets its instructions from your thoughts and beliefs. Give your subconscious the right instructions and it will take you where ever you want to go in life. When your mind is focused on your goals you direct your subconscious to create opportunities for you to achieve your goals. Your responsibility is to follow up on these opportunities.

How You Can Train Your Mind
Believe it or not I get a lot of calls and emails everyday from people who want to achieve their goals but simply can't get their mind to focus on the tasks that need to be done to have the success that they want. This happens because the mind is simply not used to focusing on your goals and following up with completing those tasks. So how do you get your mind to change? How do you train your mind?

The first step is to get the mind to stop doing what it is used to doing - or break the pattern that you've been following for so long. This will require some effort - but the reward will allow you to live the life you want and enjoy the level of success that you want.

To re-train your mind and direct your subconscious mind you start by paying more attention - so that when you see yourself getting distracted and not following up on things that you wanted to do - you take a step to break the pattern. You can break the pattern by doing something else. For example: you can start following up on what you had planned to do, you can create a list and follow up with it regularly to see if you are on track.

One thing that always works is to think about your goals every morning. As you're in bed, think about your goals and think about what you can do to achieve them during the day. If you find that you constantly say: "I don't know what do to do to achieve my goals." Then you're not looking for answers in the right place.

Take a look at what other people have done to achieve similar goals and see if you can follow the same process. For example: If you want to make more money take a look at someone else who has made a lot of money and see what they've done. Can you follow their process? Maybe you can even talk to them about the process? If you want to meet someone and be in a healthy relationship, talk to a friend who is in a successful relationship and find out what they did. By doing the above exercises you train your mind to focus on finding solutions while at the same time you direct your subconscious mind to create the opportunities for you to succeed. And - you begin to create a new pattern of thinking and you start to train the mind to work differently. You're now telling your driver where you want to go. This eliminates the confusion and allows you to achieve your goals.

You're not going to magically get your mind to focus or concentrate without you taking some form of action. When you finally do take some action your mind will still resist - but as you continue taking action the resistance will subside - REPITITION. So what action can you take? First start with the exercise I just outlined above. Next - meditate. Meditation is one of the best ways to relax and calm your mind while training it to focus on what you want. When you meditate you actually start to clear the clutter that dominates your mind.

Make the Time
Finally it seems a lot of people have come to believe that they just don't have the time to achieve their goals. If you are one of the many who have such a belief then you've really convinced yourself that your goals are not worthy of your time; because if they were you would make the time for them. I'm not talking about spending an entire day or even a few hours. It's only a few minutes at different intervals. Why try to get everything crammed into one hour? Why not try to think about your goals at different intervals during the day? For example: you may have a few minutes while you're taking a walk - think of your achieving your goals. You could also do this while you're taking a shower, driving, walking, anytime. Here's a suggestion; the next time you are driving or taking a shower, pay attention to your thoughts. Are these thoughts actually working for your or against you? Would it be better to focus on your goals or keep recycling the negative clutter or junk in your head? The choice is yours - and taking action is really about taking a small step. You don't need to spend hours meditating. Even if you simply mediated for 5 or 10 minutes a day you'd be able to increase your ability to concentrate and

focus by a 100-percent within a matter of days! Do it for weeks or months and you'll have dramatic results!

How to Put Your Mind to Sleep Quickly and Rest Completely

If you often lay awake, unable to put your mind to rest while you're tossing and turning, you're going to love what you're about to read, because I'm about to share with you one of the most powerful methods for quickly shutting off your mind, and drifting off to sleep.

As you may already know, your mind must be in the Alpha brain-wave stage to fall asleep. This is the stage your mind enters you're still conscious, but your body and begin to relax. It enables your more rampant and conscious mind to turn off as you enter the realm of sleep. We all know how it feels... when you're lying awake in bed trying to fall asleep, it seems like your mind is running on hyper-speed. It's almost like you're thinking 10 times faster than when you're just normally awake and alert. In fact, if you experience this often, I can tell you for a fact that your mind IS working harder than it is when you're not trying to fall asleep, and there is a very good reason for it, here's why this happens. In my books and articles on sleep, I often teach a principle: "What you focus on expands." You see, your mind responds to focus, and it goes hand in hand with the law of momentum. What is the law of momentum? Quite simply:

"Energy in motion, tends to STAY in motion"

"Energy stopped, tends to STAY stopped"

In other words, if you take action in your life, and begin to create success, you will experience more and more success every day. Success breeds success. On the other hand, if you sit your butt down on the couch to watch TV and say, "Aww, just one show, I'll only watch one show," very soon you'll be sitting there for four hours, and you'll watch five or six shows.

The law of momentum is everywhere in life, in physics, with your body, and most importantly, with your "thoughts." You see, your thinking is very predictable; it all works on the law of focus and momentum. Your mind is like a big ball of potential thinking energy, just waiting for you to give it a direction to think wildly into. It awaits and responds your every command. It's an exceptional tool except, most of us aren't very experienced at "controlling" this amazing tool. In fact, a lot people aren't even aware that they can control it! And this is where sleep problems come in.

Imagine your mind like a giant overflowing lake that's just waiting for an outlet to pour into... Slowly, when it finds an outlet, it begins with a trickle of water. That trickle turns into a stream. Then, that stream turns into a small river. Pretty soon, the small river is a giant unstoppable waterfall. Your thoughts work in the same way when you're "trying" to fall asleep.

For example, you're lying in bed, frustrated, forcing your mind to not think. "I just want to get some sleep! Stop thinking! Okay, starting now... I won't think anymore. No think... nothing. My life is nothing... If only I would finally get motivated in my job maybe I would finally create the income to start traveling instead of dealing with these problems. Problems, how can I... Ahh, I'm thinking again! Stop it!"

You get even more frustrated, and repeat the process over again in a few minutes. So how do you stop it? It's easy, you see, you can easily control your thinking, except most people aren't aware of the tools necessary! The good news is, I'm about to give you the 3-step handbook to controlling your mind. Here are the 3-universal steps that will enable you to not only stop thinking; you'll also be able to lower your brain-waves into the alpha brain-state, which will quickly let you enter sleep...

Awareness

The first step to changing anything is becoming aware that it's happening, especially if it's your mind. Pretend your mind is racing, and you finally realize that you're thinking... Most people at this stage get extremely frustrated and "try" to force the mind into submission. It doesn't work! Why? Because, what you focus on expands. The more frustrated you get, the more you're focusing on frustration, so you'll get even MORE frustration and more thinking... on and on!

So the first step is to simply become "aware" of the fact that you're thinking. Nothing more. When you notice that you're thinking, smile to yourself, and say, "I just noticed myself thinking... Interesting..." Now notice what happens inside of you when you do this... something VERY profound. If "I" just noticed "myself" thinking, perhaps there are really two completely separate identities running your life? There is the "I" and there is the "self."

The "I", is the real you, the higher being, the "I" behind the mind, that runs the show, the heart, the soul, the true conscious being, the choice maker.

The "self" is the mind; if left to run the show, it will run in endless circles until the edge of insanity.

The moment you do this, the moment you become "aware" - you are no longer a slave to your mind. You have won. After you become aware... do nothing, just lay there for 3 seconds and notice how it feels to be present in who you really are, not the mind, but you, the "I" - there is a great feeling of peace behind that presence in the "I." Why? Because when you are aware like this, you're aware of the power of your choice making. You now have the power of choice.

Relaxed Focus
"What you focus on expands." Now that you have become aware of your thinking, all you have to do is "direct" your mind into a place that will bring you into a deep, deep place of relaxation. Think about it, if before your mind will relentlessly race into any direction you give it; why not pick a direction that will give you peace and restful sleep?

But, most people don't know what that direction really is. It's really easy. If you focus on anything your body does or feels subconsciously, you will begin to become more and more realized. For example your breathing, the feeling of the pillow on your head, the sounds of nature outside (unless you live in the city), the warmth of your body. These are all things that happen, yet your conscious mind doesn't think about them.

As you know, "What you focus on expands"... So what would happen if you focused on something that is happening in your "subconscious"? That's right, your conscious thinking would diminish, and your subconscious mind would begin to take over the entire

43

process of you falling asleep! It really is that simple, and it works every-time.

The easiest one is your breathing. And I promise you if you just try this tonight, you will be shocked when you wake up in the morning: "Wow! It worked!"

Repetition

As I said, the easiest one to focus on is your breathing. In the beginning, you'll find this easier said than done. Let me walk you through it.

- Begin by taking your focus onto your breathing. Take a deep breath in. Hold it for a short while, and slowly exhale...

- Count "1"

- Breathe in again... hold it shortly, exhale slowly, and count...

- "2"

Why count? Because I guarantee you, in the very beginning, you may find it challenging to hold your focus. In fact, you'll be surprised as you may not even make it to "5" the first time. This is because your conscious ever-thinking mind will butt in and interrupt. You may randomly go off into a barrage of thoughts again. If this happens, and it very well may, what do you do?

Simply become aware, and begin focusing on your breathing again. Guess what happens? As you become aware, 2 or 3 times... your mind will give up. I guarantee you, beyond the shadow of a doubt, when you get to "10" or "15" breaths you will feel a wave of relaxation in your body. This is the silent "click" as your mind shifts from the high frequency Beta brain-waves into Alpha brain-waves. Your subconscious mind will do the rest!

*****

This section is the most important section in the book. It defines and teaches you about your mind and why you do the things you do.

But it also teaches you how to change the subconscious mind where all action/behavior/conduct occurs.

Study this chapter over and over again until it becomes set in your mind and you understand fully what it is teaching you. If you have any questions please feel free to write to me because I want you to get it right the first time: harry@epubwealth.com

Changing your behavior is not as easy as it sounds but it can be done. Think back and try to remember how you acquired as a belief system some of the things you do. If you learned the abhorrent behavior then you can unlearn them to and replace them with corrective behavior and conduct worthy of a peaceful existence.

Chapter 1 – The Mind of a Con Man

The following was taken as an excerpt from the book,
"The Mind of a Con Man"

*****

I will describe Type 1 Con Men who are professional con men that purposely prey on individuals for some type of gain – money, power, sex, etc but I will also describe Type 2 Con Men that you come into contact daily.

These people are manipulators and can be anyone from your mommy, family members, and friends to co-workers, sales people and advertisers in general. Type 2 individuals are quite different from Type 1 individuals.

Type 1 individuals are professionals at practicing their deceptive trade for pecuniary gain. Fortunately you may never come into contact with a Bernie Madoff or Frank

Abagnale but you do come into contact with Type 2 individuals daily.

These people are what I call amateur con men, who attempt to manipulate you into doing something they want you to do. Candidly, Type 2 individuals are more dangerous than Type 1 individuals.

The "con game" (the word "con" is short for "confidence") is a worldwide pandemic problem. No country or race of people is immune to the con game. Dictators are nothing more than con men deceiving whole countries into believing something they want them to believe.

Islamic fanaticism and Arab fundamentalism is the most preemptive con game going today. Using religion, Arab leaders have conned Muslims worldwide into believing a false doctrine and the blood flows red from their evil deception.

Closer to home, the con game seemingly appears nightly on the evening news and makes good copy too. Here is a recent article of what is fast becoming an epidemic of the con game within academia:

http://www.nytimes.com/2013/04/28/magazine/diederik-stapels-audacious-academic-fraud.html?nl=todaysheadlines&emc=edit_th_20130428

The article is rather long but it is a real eye-opener and one that only briefly touches on the con game within academia. You can bet there is more to uncover.

So, who is fooling who? Better yet, who is fooling YOU? We shall see so sit back for the adventure. You are never going to be the same again…

*****

Type 1 & Type 2 Con Men & The Psychology of Lying

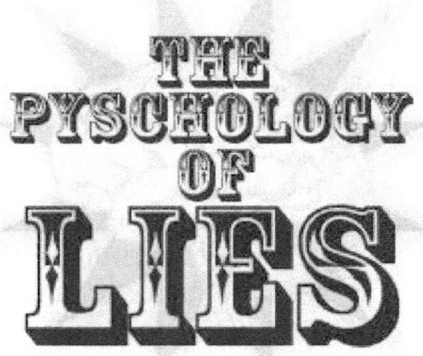

Okay, hopefully the section on "Laying a Proper Foundation" opened your mind up to learning about the human behavior of both Type 1 and Type 2 con men.

Each type has different human behavioral traits yet shares some common traits too. I will describe both in detail in this chapter. I will also get into the psychology of lying and why this is the most important trait of a con man.

Type 1 Con Men

Diabolical is defined as: "of, relating to, or characteristic of the devil: devilish <a *diabolical* plot>" and is one of the best descriptions of a con man to date.

Com men are VERY diabolical and enjoy what they do. Their actions and conduct are purposeful and deliberate and they know full well of what they are doing. They cannot hide behind some psychological disorder or claim some childhood trauma made them practice their deceptive trade.

In a court of law, they are doomed because they have no defense whatsoever. This is apparent with some of the court cases that have been reported in the media recently. Bernie Madoff received a 150 year sentence for his decades of deception and his actions left a good many people scratching their heads in wonder including his wife and family as well as the regulators and law enforcement.

Bernie Madoff knew full well what he was doing was a massive con game and lived within this game for decades even deceiving himself that he could continue it forever. Unfortunately the economy fell out and exposed him as well as numerous other con men of a lesser degree of fame and fortune.

Here is a list of Type 1 Con Men, some of whom you know and can identify but others you have never seen before:

The 10-Most Famous Con Men in History

1. Frank Abagnale [Born: 1948]

Frank Abagnale is a former cheque con artist, forger and imposter who, for five years in the 1960s, passed bad checks worth more than $2.5 million in 26 countries. The recent blockbuster film Catch Me If You Can is based on his life. His first experience of fraud was as a youth when he used his father's Mobil card to buy car parts that he would then sell back to the gas station for a lower price. He did not realize that his father was the one who had to foot the bill and when he was eventually confronted with the fraud, his mother sent him for four months to a juvenile correction facility.

After moving to New York, Frank lived solely on the income of his fraudulent activities. One of his most famous tricks was to print his own account number on fake bank deposit slips so that when clients of the bank deposited money, it would actually go in to his account. By the time the banks realized what had happened, Frank had taken $40,000 and run.

For two years, Abagnale travelled around the world free by masquerading as a Pan Am pilot. He was able to abuse the professional courtesy of other airlines to provide free transport for competing airline pilots if they had to move to another city at short notice. When he was nearly caught leaving a plane, he changed his masquerade to that of a Doctor. He worked as a medical supervisor for 11 months without detection. At other times he worked as a lawyer and a teacher.

He was eventually caught in France and spent six months in prison there. After that he was extradited to Sweden and imprisoned for a further six months. After a successful escape whilst travelling to the United States, he was finally given 12 years in Prison. He escaped from his prison by masquerading as an undercover officer of the Bureau of Prisons. He was once again captured in New York City and returned to jail. After serving only five years of his sentence, the US Federal Government offered him his freedom in return for helping the government against fraud and scam artists without pay.

He currently runs Abagnale and Associates, a financial fraud consultancy company and is a multi-millionaire.

2. Charles Ponzi [Born: 1882; Died: 1949]

Ponzi, an Italian immigrant to the United States became one of the most famous con men in American history. While many people do not know the name Ponzi, the Ponzi Scheme is extremely well known and continues today in Internet Make Money Fast schemes. His early life is not entirely known as he was prone to fabricate stories about it. What is known is that he spent a short amount of time at University in Rome and, after dropping out, caught a boat to Boston, USA where he arrived with $2.50 in his pocket.

His early years in the United States were troublesome. He began working at a restaurant but was soon fired for playing tricks with the bills and shortchanging customers. His next job was working in a bank in Canada that catered to Italian immigrants. His knowledge of numbers helped him to do very well there. Unfortunately it turned out that the owner of the bank was stealing money from newly opened savings accounts to pay the interest on the interest bearing accounts and to cover bad investments. The bank owner eventually fled to Mexico and left Ponzi without a job. After writing a fraudulent cheque and spending a number of years in prison, Ponzi determined to become wealthy at any cost.

Once he had settled in to life on the outside, he discovered postal reply coupons through a letter that was sent to him from abroad. He realized that he could buy foreign coupons at massively devalued prices (because of price fixing after the war) and then resell them in the United States for a 400% profit. This was a form of arbitrage and it was legal. Ponzi began canvasses friends and acquaintances for money – promising them a 50% return or a doubling of their money in 90 days. He started his own company, the Securities Exchange Company, to promote the scheme.

The word of this great investment quickly spread and before long Ponzi was living in a luxurious mansion. He was bringing in cash at a fantastic rate, but the simplest financial analysis showed that he wasn't making money, he was losing it rapidly. For every dollar he took in, he went more deeply into debt. As long as money kept flowing in, Ponzi would stay ahead of the eventual collapse.

People soon began to become suspicious and the press was starting to publish negative articles about him.

Inevitably people were starting to demand their money. Shortly after, federal agents raided his office and shut it down. No stock of stamps was found and everyone that had invested their money with Ponzi lost every penny. It is probably that he lost tens of millions of dollars. Ponzi plead guilty of mail fraud and was sent to prison. After one escape he was returned to jail to complete his sentence. He was eventually deported back to Italy and he died there in poverty in 1949.

3. Joseph Weil [Born: 1877; Died: 1975]

Joseph "Yellow Kid" Weil was one of the most famous con men in his era. Over the course of his career he is believed to have stolen over 8 million dollars. In his first job as a collector, he realized that his co-workers were collecting their debts but keeping a little part of the money for themselves. Weil started a protection racket – offering not to report their activities in return for a small portion of what they were taking.

He also used phony oil deals, women, fixed races, and an endless list of other tricks to steal from an increasingly gullible public. He could change his persona daily to further his gains: one day he was Dr. Henri Reuel, a noted geologist who travelled around and told his hosts that he was a representative for a big oil company while draining them of the cash they gave him to "invest in fuel." The next day he was director of the Elysium Development Company, promising land to innocent believers while robbing them in recording and abstract fees. Or he was a chemist par excellence, who had discovered how to copy dollar bills; promising to increase your fortune, he would multiply your bills then take the booty once the police arrived.

In his autobiography, Weil writes:

"The desire to get something for nothing has been very costly to many people who have dealt with me and with other con men," Weil writes. "But I have found that this is the way it works. **The average person, in my estimation, is ninety-nine per cent animal and one per cent human.** The ninety-nine per cent that is animal causes very little trouble. But the one per cent that is human causes all our woes. When people learn — as I doubt they will — that they can't get something for nothing, crime will diminish and we shall live in greater harmony."

4. Victor Lustig [Born: 1890; Died: 1947]

Victor Lustig was renowned as the Man who Sold the Eiffel Tower. He was born in Bohemia but later moved to Paris where he was able to con people on his frequent journeys between Paris and New York. His first con was to show people a device that could print $100 bills. The only problem, he would tell them, is that it only prints one bill every six hours. Many people paid him enormous amounts of money (usually over $30,000) for the device. In fact, the device contained two real hidden $100 bills – once they were spat out by the machine it would produce only blank paper. By the time the buyers discovered this, Lustig was well gone with their money.

In 1925, as France was recovering from the war, the upkeep of the Eiffel tower was an almost unbearable expense for the city of Paris. When Lustig read about this in a paper, he came up with his most brilliant idea. After forging government credentials, he invited six scrap metal dealers to a secret meeting in a hotel. He explained that the City could not afford to keep the tower and that they had to sell it for scrap. He told them the secrecy of the meeting and all future dealings was due to the fact that the public may become distressed at the idea of the removal of the tower.

While it seems implausible, at the time the tower was built it was meant to be temporary and this happened just 18 years after the original date for removal of the tower. Lustig took the dealers in a limousine to tour the tower. One of the dealers, Andre Poisson was convinced that the tale was legitimate and he handed over the money. When he realized he had been conned, he was too embarrassed to tell the police and Lustig escaped with the money. One month later, he returned to Paris to try the whole scam again. This time it was reported to the police but Lustig managed to escape.

At one point, Lustig convinced Al Capone to invest $50,000 with him. He stored the money in a vault and returned it two months later, stating that the deal had fallen through. Capone, so impressed by Lustig's honesty gave him $5,000 for his effort. In 1934, Lustig was found guilty of counterfeiting. He pled guilty and was sentenced to 20 years in Alcatraz. In 1947 he died of pneumonia whilst in jail in Springfield, Missouri.

5. George Parker [Born: 1870; Died: 1936]

Parker was one of the most audacious con men in American history. He made his living selling New York's public landmarks to unwary tourists. His favorite object for sale was the Brooklyn Bridge, which he sold twice a week for years. He convinced his marks that they could make a fortune by controlling access to the roadway. More than once police had to remove naive buyers from the bridge as they tried to erect toll barriers.

Other public landmarks he sold included the original Madison Square Garden, the Metropolitan Museum of Art, Grant's Tomb, and the Statue of Liberty. George had many different methods for making his sales. When he sold Grant's Tomb, he would often pose as the general's grandson. He even set up a fake "office" to handle his real estate swindles. He produced impressive forged documents to prove that he was the legal owner of whatever property he was selling.

Parker was convicted of fraud three times. After his third conviction on December 17th, 1928 he was sentenced to a life term at Sing Sing Prison. He spent the last eight years of his life behind bars. He was popular among guards and fellow inmates who enjoyed hearing of his exploits. George is remembered as one of the most successful con men in the history of the United States, as well as one of history's most talented hoaxers. His exploits have passed into popular culture, giving rise to phrases such as "and if you believe that, I have a bridge to sell you", a popular way of expressing a belief that someone is gullible.

6. Soapy Smith [Born: 1860; Died: 1898]

Soapy Smith (born Jefferson Randolph Smith) was an American con artist and gangster who had a major hand in the organized criminal operations of Denver, Colorado, Creede, Colorado, and Skagway, Alaska from 1879 to 1898. He is perhaps the most famous "sure-thing" bunko man of the old west. Sometime in the late 1870s or early 1880s, Smith began duping entire crowds with a ploy the Denver newspapers dubbed The Prize Package Soap Sell Swindle.

Jefferson would open his "tripe and keister" (display case on a tripod) on a busy street corner. Piling ordinary soap cakes onto the keister top, he would describe their wonders. As he spoke to the growing crowd of curious onlookers, he would pull out his wallet and begin wrapping paper money ranging from one dollar up to one hundred dollars, around a select few of the bars. He then finished each bar by wrapping plain paper around it to hide the money. He mixed the money-wrapped packages in with wrapped bars containing no money. He then sold the soap to the crowd for a dollar a cake.

A shill planted in the crowd would buy a bar, tear it open it, and loudly proclaim that he had won some money, waving it around for all to see. This performance had the desired effect of enticing the sale of the packages. More often than not, victims bought several bars before the sale was completed. Midway through the sale, Smith would announce that the hundred-dollar bill still remained in the pile, unpurchased. He then would auction off the remaining soap bars to the highest bidders.

Through the masterful art of manipulation and sleight-of-hand, the cakes of soap wrapped with money were hidden and replaced with packages holding no cash. It was assured that the only money "won" went to members of what became known as the "Soap Gang." Soapy was eventually shot to death by a group he swindled in a card game.

7. Eduardo de Valfierno

Eduardo de Valfierno, who referred to himself as Marqués (marquis), was an Argentine con man who allegedly masterminded the theft of the Mona Lisa. Valfierno paid several men to steal the work of art from the Louvre, including museum employee Vincenzo Peruggia. On August 21, 1911 Peruggia hid the Mona Lisa under his coat and simply walked out the door.

Before the heist took place, Valfierno commissioned French art restorer and forger Yves Chaudron to make six copies of the Mona Lisa. The forgeries were then shipped to various parts of the world, readying them for the buyers he had lined up. Valfierno knew once the Mona Lisa was stolen it would be harder to smuggle copies past customs. After the heist the copies were delivered to their buyers, each thinking they had the original which had just been stolen for them. Because Valfierno just wanted to sell forgeries, he only needed the original Mona Lisa to disappear and never contacted Peruggia again after the crime. Eventually Peruggia was caught trying to sell the painting and it was returned to the Louvre in 1913.

8. James Hogue [Born: 1959]

Hogue is a US impostor who most famously entered Princeton University by posing as a self-taught orphan. In 1986 Hogue enrolled in a Palo Alto High School as Jay Mitchell Huntsman, a 16-year-old orphan from Nevada. He had adopted the identity of a dead infant. A suspicious local reporter exposed him. In 1988 Hogue enrolled at Princeton University using the alias Alexi Indris Santana, a self-taught orphan from Utah. He deferred admission for one year because he had been convicted of the theft of bicycle frames in Utah. Hogue claimed in his application materials that he had slept outside in the Grand Canyon, raising sheep and reading philosophers. He violated his parole to enter class. For the next two years he lived as Santana and as a member of the track team. He was also admitted into the Ivy Club.

In 1991 Hogue's real identity was exposed when Renee Pacheco, a student from the Palo Alto High School, recognized him. He was arrested for defrauding the university for $30,000 in financial aid and sentenced to three years in jail with 5-years probation and 100 hours of community service.

On May 16, 1993 Hogue made headlines again through his association with Harvard University. Having lied about his identity again, he was able to take a job as a security guard in one of Harvard's on campus museums. A few months into his tenure, museum officials noticed that several gemstones on exhibit had been replaced with inexpensive fakes. Somerville police seized Hogue in his home and charged him with grand larceny to the tune of $50,000.

On March 12, 2007 Hogue pleaded guilty to a single felony count of theft of more than $15,000 in exchange for a prison sentence not to exceed 10 years, and prosecutors' agreement to drop other theft and habitual criminal charges.

9. Robert Hendy-Freegard [Born: 1971]

Robert Hendy-Freegard is a British barman, car salesman, conman and impostor who masqueraded as an MI5 agent and fooled several people to go underground for fear of IRA assassination. He met his victims on social occasions or as customers in the pub or car dealership where he was working. He would reveal his "role" as an undercover agent for MI5, Special Branch or Scotland Yard working against the IRA. He would win them over, ask for money and make them do his bidding. He demanded that they cut off contact with family and friends, go through "loyalty tests" and live alone in poor conditions. He seduced five women, claiming that he wanted to marry them. Initially some of the victims refused to co-operate with the police because he had warned them that police would be double agents or MI5 agents performing another "loyalty test".

Hendy-Freegard also seduced a newly married personal assistant who was taking care of his children. He told her he was with MI5 and forced her to cut contact with friends and family lest the IRA would kill her. He also took naked pictures of her and threatened to give them to her husband if she would not cooperate. She had to change her name and tell the deed poll officer it was because she was sexually abused as a child. Her loyalty tests included sleeping in Heathrow airport and on park benches for several nights and pretending to be a Jehovah's Witness so that his bosses in MI5 would let them marry.

In 2002 Scotland Yard and the FBI organized a sting operation. First, the FBI bugged the phone of the American psychologist's parents. Her mother told Hendy-Freegard she would hand over £10,000 but only in person. Hendy-Freegard met the mother in Heathrow airport where police apprehended him. He denied all charges and claimed they were part of a conspiracy against him and continued this story in the subsequent trial. On June 23, 2005, after an eight month trial, Blackfriars Crown Court convicted Robert Hendy-Freegard for two counts of kidnapping, 10 of theft and 8 of deception. On September 6, 2005 he was given a life sentence. Police doubt that they have discovered all the victims. On April 25, 2007, the BBC reported that Robert Hendy-Freegard had appealed against his kidnapping convictions and won. This means that the life sentence is revoked but he will still serve nine years for the other offences. He could be free by the end of 2007.

10. Bernard Cornfeld [Born: 1927; Died: 1995]

Bernard Cornfeld was a prominent businessman and international financier who sold investments in US mutual funds. He was born in Turkey. When he moved to the US, he first worked as a social worker but became a mutual fund salesman in the 1950s. Although he suffered from a stammer, he had a natural gift for selling and when a schoolfriend's father died, the two of them used the $3,000 insurance money to purchase and run an age and weight guessing stand at the Coney Island funfair.

In the 1960s, Cornfeld formed his own mutual fund selling company, Investors Overseas Services (IOS), which he incorporated outside the US with funds in Canada and headquarters in Geneva, Switzerland. Although the headquarters were officially in Geneva, the main operational offices of IOS were in Ferney-Voltaire, France, a short drive from the Swiss border to Geneva— this was simply a means of avoiding the problems of obtaining Swiss work-permits for the many employees. During the next ten years, IOS raised in excess of $2.5 billion, bringing Cornfeld a personal fortune of more than $100 million. Cornfeld himself became known for conspicuous consumption with lavish parties. Socially, he was generous and jovial.

A group of 300 IOS employees complained to the Swiss authorities that Cornfeld and his co-founders pocketed part of the proceeds of a share issue raised among employees in 1969. Consequently he was charged with fraud in 1973 by the Swiss authorities. When Cornfeld visited Geneva, Swiss authorities arrested him. He served 11 months in a Swiss jail before being freed on a bail surety of $600,000. He returned to Beverly Hills, living less ostentatiously than in his previous years. He developed an obsession for health foods and vitamins, renounced red meat and seldom drank alcohol. He suffered a stroke and died of a cerebral aneurysm on 27th February 1995 in London, England.

Con Men Living Today

- **Frank Abagnale** (1948): U.S. check forger and impostor; his autobiography was made into the movie *Catch Me If You Can.*
- **Sergio Cragnotti** (1940): Former Italian industrialist and president of a football team who masterminded the Cirio bankruptcy.
- **Marc Dreier** (1950): Founder of attorney firm Dreier LLP. Convicted of selling approximately $700 million worth of fictitious promissory notes, and other crimes.
- **Kevin Foster** (1958/59): British investment fraudster convicted of running a Ponzi scheme.
- **Robert Hendy-Freegard** (1971): Briton who kidnapped people by impersonating an MI5 agent and conned them out of money.
- **James Arthur Hogue** (1959): U.S. impostor who most famously entered Princeton University by posing as a self-taught orphan
- **Sante Kimes:** Convicted of fraud, robbery, murder, and over 100 other crimes
- **Matt the Knife** (1981): American-born con artist, card cheat and pickpocket who, from the ages of approximately 14 through 21, bilked dozens of casinos, corporations and at least one Mafia crime family.
- **Steven Kunes** (1956): Former television screenwriter with convictions for forgery, grand

theft, and false use of financial information. In 1982 he attempted to sell a faked interview with J. D. Salinger to *People* magazine.

- **Bernard Madoff** (1938): Former American stock broker and non-executive chairman of the NASDAQ stock market who admitted to the operation of the largest Ponzi scheme in history.
- **Barry Minkow** (1967): Known for the *ZZZZ Best* scam.
- **Richard Allen Minsky** (1944): Scammed female victims for sex by pretending to be jailed family members over the phone.
- **Lou Pearlman** (1954): Former boy band impresario, convicted for perpetrating a large and long-running Ponzi scheme.
- Steven Jay Russell (1957): Georgia deputy police officer who impersonated several individuals to escape from a Texas prison, and embezzled over hundreds of thousands of dollars from the North American Medical Management corporation. Best known for pretending to be dying from AIDS in order to transfer out of prison, only to be caught after later trying to appeal his life-partner Phillip Morris' jail sentence. Inspired a movie titled: "I Love You Phillip Morris"
- **Calisto Tanzi** (1938): Former Italian industrialist and president of Parmalat, which he led to one of the costliest bankruptcies in history.
- **Kevin Trudeau** (1963): US writer and billiards promoter convicted of fraud and larceny, known for late-night infomercials and books about "Natural Cures 'They' Don't Want You to Know About".

*****

One important factor to remember when it comes to Type 1 con men is that all of their actions are deliberate and purposeful. They all know they are conning people and they all know that they are in it for pecuniary gain.

The criminal mind has convinced itself that getting something for nothing is better than getting it in a lawful manner.

Con men believe that they are superior to other people, and that others simply don't have the intelligence to catch them. They have no empathy or compassion for anything.

In studies conducted by my Applied Mind Sciences lab using captured and imprisoned con men we did discover that 6 out of 10 con men have a very high intelligence quotient (IQ). The other 4 had average intelligence and all four claimed that they got into the con game by accident and were trying to make things right before they got caught. Interesting ,eh? Remorse is a funny thing; remorse comes after a person is caught but never comes up during the con game.

The fact of the matter is that the majority of con men view other people as sheep to be herded and conned. They have no regard whatsoever of the damage they do and the lives they ruin and they simply do not care. Why they do this will be discussed in more detail in Chapter 3.

Now let's discuss Type 2 individuals...

Type 2 Individuals

I call Type 2 people "individuals" rather than con men for the simple fact that many Type 2 individuals are not purposeful in their actions to committing a crime. The ARE purposeful in their actions to manipulate but not insofar as for the purpose of pecuniary gain in any form.

Type 2 individuals are manipulators and some are very good at it and practice it daily. There manipulators can be anyone from your mommy, other family members, friends, co-workers and more.

They hide their actions behind the facade of only "trying to help" when in reality, they are "only trying to harm."

They are not diabolical but they are immature and hurtful in their actions. The reasons behind their actions are as varied as the individuals themselves and depending on the relationship; the reasons can be jealousy, hate, envy, revenge, enjoyment in hurting others, and wanting to bring others down to their level, and more…

Like I stated in my introduction, chances are that you may never come in contact with a Type 1 con man, but you do come in contact with Type 2 individuals daily and this is why I consider Type 2 individuals more dangerous.

The fact of the matter is that with the advent of the Internet and having information at your fingertips, people allow others to do their thinking.

I had a staff manager and co-worker years ago that was a master manipulator and always used the saying, "I didn't hire you to think; I will do your thinking for you."

When I pointed out that this was not the way to manage my people, her response was, "It works for me and I have managed this way for years."

Candidly, I was dumbfounded by her response and just looked at her before I replied, "What has worked for you? You have been married three times, your kids don't even talk to you, you have the highest employee turnover in the company and I can bet even your dog hates your guts."

She then stated emphatically that I could not talk to her in that manner and stormed away so I fired her.

She then filed a lawsuit against me and the company, which she lost horribly and to this day, has never been hired by another company in a managerial position.

In essence, this woman was deceiving herself and self-deception is the worst form of deception.

The Psychology of Lying

One of the most perplexing human conditions is why people find a need to lie, cheat and deceive.

Deception has become a lifestyle and more people spend their lives within a web of deception than outside of it.

They have built whole worlds within their existences and many have no idea how it occurred or how to stop it.

In this book, I want to address the subject of lies, cheats and deception in detail and I am quite certain you will be amazed.

One would think that les, cheating and deception are really one-in-the-same but they are not and like I said, you will be amazed at just how distinct the reasons behind all three really are and how compelling they are to break.

Noah Pranksky

In the book, "Man Up - The Decline & Fall of Manhood" Dr. Noah Pranksky defines the decline of manhood with the main cause being deception.

Female Wolf Packs

Noah Pranksky

Furthermore, in another of his books, "Female Wolf Packs" he demonstrates the problems men have with women and the leading problem is deception.

The problem of "trust' between genders has become so severe that each gender is literally giving up on relationships and going off to form family units without the opposite gender in the picture.

Women are using the services of sperm banks to sire children and men are choosing surrogate mothers.

The question of "why" has been a part of the conscience of man since the dawn of time.

It has caused us to seek answers, better solutions, invention, progress, increased knowledge and more.

But more often than not, most of our questions of "why" now centers on personal behavioral traits and habits that perplex us and cause us consternation and regret.

Candidly, most people have no idea why they do the things they do so in this book I am going to explain in detail why you lie, cheat and deceive and how to overcome these perplexing problems.

> Me, I'm dishonest, and you can always trust a dishonest man to be dishonest. Honestly, it's the honest ones you have to watch out for.
> **Johnny Depp**

Where is the gain for people who lie, cheat and deceive? This is an important question to ask too.

In Chapter 1, I explained the difference between true reality that the conscious mind SEES and the PERCEIVED reality that the subconscious mind uses. There is a difference and the difference is quite large.

A liar, cheater and deceiver does perceive a big gain in their behavior, otherwise they would not do what they do. This perception is a wrongful belief system and hence; their gain is a false gain.

But candidly, even a false gain is worthy of their actions even if this appears silly on the surface. In essence the very first person they deceive is themselves.

In the book, "The Greatest Fraud the World Has Ever Known," it goes to the root of the problem of self deception.

"The Greatest Fraud the World Has Ever Known" is the person practicing deception because they are only fooling themselves into believing that this is a lifestyle worth pursuing.

Here is an excerpt from the book…

In today's world, fraud is running rampant. But in actuality, fraud is not new concept. From the beginning of time man has used deception from everything such as war to love.

In the animal kingdom, animals use deception for protection by the use of camouflage and more.

The high technology of our times makes access to all forms of information almost instantaneous and the news media sensationalizes fraud to a point of frenzy.

Fraud is defined as intentional deception made for personal gain or to damage another individual.

In recent years, top fraudsters such as Bernie Madoff, Ken Lay and Jeff Skilling of Enron, Allen Stanford, Bernie Ebbers of Worldcom, Dennis Kozlowski of Tyco International, Martin Frankel, James Lewis, Lou Pearlman of N'Sync fame, Barry Minkow of ZZZZ Best, and Tom Petters have been brought to justice and given lengthy prison terms.

No one seemingly escapes fraud; everyone on the planet has been deceived in some manner.

As Chief Forensics Investigator for ForensicsNation.com, I compile and preserve evidence of cyber-crime fraud all the time.

Cyber crime is rampant too and growing; you would not believe how exposed the average citizen is today.

Society has come to rely on computers, cell phones, and computer-run public systems such as traffic lights, food distribution, water supply and much more in such a way that any disruption of these services jeopardizes our quality of life.

People make use of Wi-Fi systems inside their homes, in public places such as libraries and Starbucks, which make them huge targets for hackers and crackers.

As a behavioral scientist, I have studied the criminal mind and have made many conclusions.

Recently we busted a voyeur using a wireless camera to spy on a Hooters waitress while she was undressing in her apartment. We caught him a couple of blocks away in his car with a handheld viewing device.

When I played back what he had seen for the waitress, her comment was, "Why? He could see more on the Internet."

And yes, it is true, you can Google just about any body part you want and see more on the Internet but the waitress missed the one important factor that causes crime - the thrill of getting away with something that is forbidden!

When a person thinks of fraud, rarely do they ever think along the lines of defrauding themselves but yet this is the most common occurrences of fraud.

Self deception runs rampant in our respective psyches; the ability to deceive ourselves cannot be minimized.

This book addresses this self deception and our inherent need to defraud ourselves.

We defraud ourselves in many ways; too many to list here but here is a partial list: the way we eat, how much we eat, our diets in general, our looks, our need to be loved, sex, our need to achieve, our beliefs, and more.

The total essences of our lives are completely affected by self deception; most of our personal existences cannot be lived without the deceptions we have created.

Let me give you an example: A person buys an automobile that they really cannot afford because it provides a status symbol of success. In many people's minds, a high-priced automobile means they "made it" but the reality is they haven't made it at all unless you count making themselves a slave to the monthly bill that pays for the automobile.

The reality of the high monthly payment takes a back seat to the perception of the automobile being a status symbol.

People overeat to assuage some pain due to stress and anxiety. They deceive themselves into believing that eating takes their minds off their problems.

They lie, gossip and deceive because it brings others that they perceive are above them down to their level.

This is the main cause of bullying and malicious gossip. We all do it; maybe not to a point where something really bad occurs like suicide, but we all still do it.

Without a doubt, we deceive ourselves the most when it comes to looks and beauty. Everything from anorexia to tanning to the clothes we wear top the list of self deception due to concerns over how a person looks.

Why are physical things leading the list of self deceptions? Why aren't the mental things at the top? After all, all of our self deceptions originate in the subconscious mind.

In this book, I will attempt to answer these questions and more. I will examine our need for self deception and the results of practicing this interesting human trait.

I will offer examples for you to ponder and that will demonstrate the core essential of my premises. None of what I present must be taken as a given; deception is subjective, which means it becomes anything you want it to become.

What is objective here is studying my core essential premises and weighing them against your own existence. A thorough and object examination of yourself may become painful but you will quickly realize that your own self deceptions rob you of a quiet and peaceful existence.

One objective fact is quite persistent throughout this book - The Greatest Fraud the World Has Ever Known is YOU!

Self-Deception is rampant and it isn't going to go away as long as the person practicing it perceives it as something of value.

It is quite easy to deceive yourself and a person can rationalize this deception in so many ways that it literally boggles the mind. Even with the facts known and presented to the person, the urge and need to keep the deception going is huge.

Let me give you an example…

Recently on Amazon.com I was personally attacked in the Amazon forum by a "gang" of people that had appointed themselves as Amazon Review Cops. They were harassing authors claiming that their reviews of their books were faked and they were paid reviews. They went on to accuse me as being a "paid reviewer" because I write a good many reviews.

No amount of reasoning appeased these people so I reported them to Amazon along with a plethora of authors that they had also attacked. I then filed criminal stalking charges and a federal district lawsuit for damages.

You should have heard the howl and the cry from this gang of people. They wrote to Amazon to complain that I had targeted them and was being unfair by filing criminal charges and a civil lawsuit.

Amazon's response was to tell them not to harass authors with unfounded accusations or in other words…tough, you are on your own.

Now, this gang perceived they were doing good when all they were doing was putting on a false front for what they really wanted to do, which was harass authors. They cared nothing about the reviews; they only wanted the authors to engage them in the forum where this gang could literally "tear them apart' and ruin their brand and reputation.

What they didn't expect was ME! This "homey" don't play no games and this gang never even considered the consequences of an author fighting back. It was so shocking to them that the majority of the gang wrote to me apologizing for their actions and asking to be removed from the suit. My response: "NO WAY!" Each gang member is accountable for their actions and they will pay the price for ruining brands and reputations. BTW – I had given them fair warning that if they continued in their behavior that I would file a criminal complaint and civil lawsuit; they just didn't believe it.

Here is my point and it is a big one: a person IS ALWAYS accountable for their actions and even if you deceive yourself into believing that your actions are justified then be prepared to defend yourself in a court of law. You are not invisible on the Internet.

*****

Living In a Fantasy World

Now I want to identify the main cause and reason behind con men and manipulators. It is living a fantasy life as if it were real.

In the best-selling book, "Fantasy is Easy-Everything Is Perfect, Behavioral science looks at people who live their lives within a fantasy" I outline in detail how a fantasy life destroys a person's existence.

It is a known fact within the research confines of behavioral science that the human subconscious mind cannot tell the difference between fantasy and reality. For example: your conscious mind knows that you are sitting in a movie theater watching a movie but your subconscious mind does not and when a sad scene comers along, you respond with the same emotions as if the scene was real...maybe you cry, get angry, or simply melancholy.

There has been as good many news stories recently dealing with people that have committed horrible crimes – Sandy Hook Elementary School, Aurora, CO Movie Theater killings, etc – and the questions usually raised first deal with violent video games, and the things that may have influenced behavior or cause these acts of violence. Is this true? We shall see...

Is Fantasy a Bad Thing?

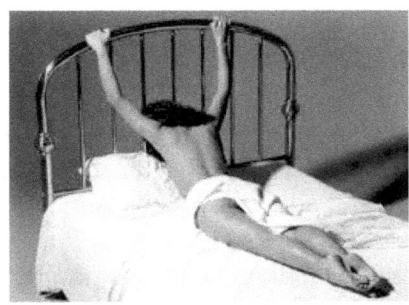

I have been a behavioral scientist for over 32-years and I am the Chief Research Scientist at Applied Mind Sciences and the question I am asked the most is this: "Is Fantasy a Bad Thing?"

So here is my answer and listen closely because it is a qualified answer: "There is good fantasy and there is bad fantasy but ANY fantasy whether good or bad that causes an individual to walk up and down within this fantasy and that manifests itself as outward behavior is BAD."

A good fantasy is one that causes you to grow as a person. Years ago I took ballroom dancing lessons and would picture myself on the dance floor mimicking the dance steps that my instructor taught me. This is an example of a good fantasy and believe me it is FANTASY since today I suck as a ballroom dancer (lol).

But let me give you a more poignant example. Many years ago I was assigned a patient that had been arrested in Las Vegas for impersonating a general flag officer of the US Military. The US Military had been aware of this man's actions for some time but when he showed up at Nellis Air Force Base, which is located on the outskirts of Las Vegas, they had him arrested.

This poor guy was really messed up. When I went to visit him at Clark County Detention Center, he demanded that I stand at attention and address him as "sir".

When I eventually made contact with his family, they were completely dumbfounded over his behavior. He had always been a loving husband and father, worked his job as an insurance executive for over 20-years, had never been in trouble before; not even a parking ticket. Then – WHAMO – out of the blue he pulls this stunt and is arrested.

I worked with this man for almost a year; got the charges dropped in return for him going through treatment, and I learned some extraordinary things from interviewing this man.

When this man was 18-years old he applied for service in the US Army but was rejected because of a perforated eardrum. He really had wanted to join the US Army and the rejection was apparently way too much for his young mind to handle so he began a "secret' fantasy of being in the US Army and he was the best soldier the world had ever seen.

In his fantasy as in all fantasies, everything is perfect. You are always the best looking person, the most admired, you are never sick or have a bad hair day, and you can do anything and everything, and so on.

In fact, after hundreds of hours of interviews with this man, if he could write a sentence he could have become one of the best action/adventure novelists on the planet; some of his stories were very exciting adventures.

It is important to note that his family knew none of this; his fantasy was truly a secret. Most people that pass you on the street daily are living their lives within some type of fantasy and their fantasies are secret too and for the most part harmless unless the fantasy begins to manifest itself in outward behavior.

So why do people do this? And even if the fantasy life of an individual does not manifest itself in outward behavior, is there any harm in living a fantasy life?

Allow me to answer the first question, "Why do people do this?" The answer is fairly obvious; they do it because, in their minds, they cannot achieve their fantasy in real life. It is also an extreme form of self-entertainment that can easily spin out of control.

In today's tough economic climate you have a plethora of situations that people feel helpless to control. College students graduating have no jobs to go to and more often than not a huge student loan debt to pay off. The American Dream has failed these young people.

Companies are downsizing and layoffs are all too common. And even as economic conditions improve, many companies have found they do not need to rehire these people that they did quite well without them.

Relationships are faltering. Young men and women are giving up on finding meaningful relationships and mates and are going off by themselves to build their lives alone.

In actuality, the list is endless and as the reasons stack up so do the fantasy lives for those who can still dream of being what they always wanted to be.

Now to the second question, "And even if the fantasy life of an individual does not manifest itself in outward behavior, is there any harm in living a fantasy life?"

The short answer is "yes" but more than likely not for the reasons you probably surmise.

Fantasy life is free; there is no effort expended, no money changes hands for training, and there is no recourse within a fantasy because everything is perfect. BUT, as the world defines, "Everything has a cost," and the cost an individual pays is that he/she gives up in reality attempting to acquire their dream/goal.

And why not? You can become anything you want in a fantasy but there are no guarantees offered in real life. And remember, fantasies are free; in real life there are costs to become anything. Time is investment, money paid in fees, tuition, books, and more.

I want to take it one step further…look at the picture under the Chapter heading above. It shows a woman tied to a bed frame. This is the result of a fantasy life that has spiraled down into the pit of depravity.

The human mind will ALWAYS seek depravity unless checked by parents, friends, the law, and social mores, etc. This why pornography is bad; if left unchecked, lust seeks a bigger and greater thrill that can lead ultimately to a serial killer or serial rapist. Step-by-step it spirals down into the pit of depravity.

In the next chapter, I am going to delve deeper into this depravity and demonstrate how erratic and violent behavior can be a result of bad fantasy.

Causes of Manifested Behavior Other Than Mental Disease

It is easy to blame mental disease for a plethora of manifested behaviors and in many cases this would be true but not always.

It makes a good defense in court but many cases claiming mental incompetence are being shot down by psychologist as being shams.

I want to now examine other causes of manifested behavior stemming from living a life within a fantasy.

I made a list and I will expand on this list as we go along…

- **Childhood Causes** – these are causes that develop within the course of a person's upbringing. It takes into account many of the factors listed below including childhood trauma, maturity, and environment. How we are raised, where we are raised and what type of an environment we are raised in all play a factor in a person's eventual adult existence.

- **Childhood Trauma** – a good many children suffer from many types of childhood traumas including physical and verbal abuse, molestation, bullying, disease, and more. These traumas can manifest themselves immediately or later on in adult life.

- **Child Rearing** – the way we are raised bears a good deal on how and what we become in our adult lives. Economic conditions have forced both parents into the workplace and children are left to themselves or day care facilities. The home environment contributes heavily to the problem especially if parents often fight because of finances, poor marital relations or whatever causes a tenuous home environment.

- **Maturity** – this is probably one of the most contributing factors to embracing a fantasy life since a person's maturity level bears a direct influence on how a person handles all situations in life. Remember, it is easy to be drawn into a fantasy life because everything in a fantasy life is perfect and free.

- **Mimicking Behavior Patterns -** A child that grows up in a home of violence tends to be violent. Parents that smoke and drink tend to raise children that exhibit the same behavior. Children will observe and mimic all types of behavior that they see their parents do as well as other adults and children. If left unchecked, these behavioral patterns can become set for life.

- **Environment** – the environment in which we are raised and live is the second most important factor contributing to the withdrawal into a fantasy life. It is easy to retreat into a world that the person deems as perfect. We tend to dream of the perfect but live in the flawed!! If we cannot change our physical environment then we can withdraw into a world that is far more satisfying than the one we actually live in.

- **Self-Entertainment** – this is a contributing factor that cannot be dismissed since I see it occurring almost daily. In the past, we called it daydreaming and it was deemed seemingly innocuous. Today, we now know that this trait is practiced by individuals far more often than first believed. It has become the scourge of the workplace as individuals withdraw into their own worlds leaving workloads untouched. Young people complain that the opposite gender only wants entertainment and fun with no commitment. Many complain that the opposite gender is in a world unto themselves and in many cases this is true.

- **Pathological Liars** – this is not a matter of low self-esteem; in fact it usually is a case of too much self-esteem. And more and more cases are being recorded where the individual lies but is not considered a pathological liar. Everybody lies; this is a given, but the reasons behind the lie determine the extent of which a person will go to keep his fantasy life going. In this case, the fantasy life is most important. Let me give you an example: I am going to tell you a lie right now. Ready? I am the King of France! Now you know this is a lie; France no longer has a monarchy. And I know that you know I am lying but I don't care because I am not in your world of reality; I am in my fantasy world and in my world I rule as king.

It is important to note that the factors cited above can also contribute to a very satisfying and mentally sound adult life too.

The door swings both ways.

I now want to discuss a human trait that stems directly from our life of fantasy…BLAME!

Blame sucks and it sucks big time…

Blame Is A Useless Concept!

The cause of blame stems directly from our lives lived within our fantasies, where everything is perfect including you. But we all know in reality we are not perfect and as Nathaniel Hawthorne states in his book, "The Scarlet letter,' we are all broken pots.

But blame is a good example of manifested behavior spilling over from our fantasy existence. We cannot be at fault since we are perfect so others must be the cause. Blame is an excuse when all we really have are choices.

THE STORY OF STUPID

Life is tough!
It's tougher if you are stupid!

Dr. Harry Jay

In my book "The Story of Stupid" I make this statement, "Life is tough; it's tougher if you are stupid." My statement isn't meant to be a putdown either. People have a tendency to making their lives tougher than what is warranted by living a lifestyle that is constantly in blame mode.

I have spent a good deal of my time in court for the sake of my patients. You only have to sit there and listen to the excuses defendants use in order to get released from charges or get bail. Some of these court sessions are better than comedy television. The defendant rarely admits to being at fault; but they have no compunction in blaming others for their deeds.

But like I said, we are all broken pots. We all have certain gifts and talents but many choose to envy the gifts and talents of others and blame their maladies on a variety of circumstances.

I can't sing and you know I can't dance and I don't look like Brad Pitt…sigh! I am just me and I have grown to accept me because no one does "ME" better than me!

I put myself through college as a standup comic and I can make people laugh and I have one of those personalities that think even gangrene is funny. My point is that you develop the talents you have been given and if you do this there is no reason to blame.

But in reality, there are a good many things we cannot become; and as people strive to become things they cannot or should not become, a certain envy develops and mostly from a lack of maturity described in Chapter 4. When this occurs, a person resorts to the blame game.

In consumerism, we have a similar situation occur which is called "scarcity thought". A person perceives that other people are getting what belongs to them and they want their issue. When they can't have what they perceive as theirs, they blame others for their lack.

The results of scarcity thought are massive consumer debt and financial meltdown into bankruptcy. Trying to keep up with the Joneses just doesn't work.

Next we have self-blame where we blame ourselves for things that occur in our lives that in reality, we didn't cause. Women are especially good at self-blame. A wife will blame herself when her mate strays into infidelity telling herself that she isn't pretty enough or sexy enough when in reality, the entire blame belongs solely to her husband. Infidelity is the result of a person embracing a lustful lifestyle and this is a person that really doesn't know what love is. And guess where lust is born? Yep, in a fantasy life!!!

There is another type of insidious blame that is the worst kind of blame. I call it "silent blame" and this is where a person harbors subconscious blame against another individual that doesn't necessarily manifest itself in outward behavior.

I had a patient that harbored ill feelings against her mother and blamed her for the breakup of a teenage relationship. A few years later she discovered her mother had nothing to do with her boyfriend breaking up with her but she still subconsciously blamed her mother because she couldn't accept the truth.

Outwardly she displayed a loving relationship with her mother but inwardly she harbored wrongful feelings. This resulted in low self-esteem and wrongful relationships that didn't last. She had been married three times and none of her marriages were long term. In other words, the manifested outward behavior was not against her mother but against her.

In working with her, I had to peel back the layers of her subconscious mind to find the root cause and she was amazed at what we both discovered in therapy sessions. Armed with the truth, she was able to finally put the resentment to rest.

I have taught you a lot of stuff and I know it can be overwhelming so you will need to re-read this book over and over again and commit it to memory but now let me sum it all up and define for you what I call the "Thoughts of a Fool" and is taken from the book of the same title.

*****

Thoughts of a Fool

Ah, the good life and what a life it would be if only we had the good life. But what is the good life? And how do we acquire it? And can this have anything to do with a con man's thinking that causes him/her to practice the con game?

Ancient Wisdom for Good Living

"What is the good life?" is a question as old as philosophy itself. In fact, it is the question that birthed philosophy as we know it. (1) Posed by ancient Greek thinkers and incorporated into the thought of Socrates through Plato, and then Aristotle, this question gets at the heart of human meaning and purpose. Why are we here, and since we are here, what are we to be doing? What is our meaning and purpose?

Out of the early Greek quest for the answer emerged two schools of thought. From Plato emerged rationalism: the good life consists of ascertaining unchanging ideals—justice, truth, goodness, beauty—those "forms" found in the ideal world. From Aristotle emerged empiricism: the good life consists of ascertaining knowledge through experience—what we can perceive of this world through our senses. (2)

For both Aristotle and Plato, rational thought used in contemplation of ideas is the substance of the good life. Despite the obvious emphasis by both on goodness emerging from the contemplative life of the mind (even though they disagreed on the source of rationality) both philosophers saw the good life as impacting and

93

benefiting society. For Plato, society must emulate justice, truth, goodness, and beauty, so he constructs an ideal society. For Aristotle, virtue lived out in society is the substance of the good life, and well-being arises from well-doing.

Not long ago, I conducted an internet search on the tag "What is the good life?" and I was amazed at what came up as the top results of my search. Most of the entries involved shopping or consumption of one variety or another. Some entries were on locations to live, and still others involved self-help books or other media aimed at helping one construct a good life. Others were the names of stores selling goods to promote "the good life." There were no immediate entries on Plato, Aristotle, or the philosophical quest that they helped inaugurate. There were no results on wisdom or the quest for knowledge lived out in a virtuous life. Instead, most of the entries involved material pursuits and gains. Sadly, this reflects our modern definition of what is good.

Perhaps, what are for many individuals still very trying economic times; it is difficult not to equate material items with the good life, more money, more security, or more opportunity. While it has always been said of every generation that these are times of great crisis and upheaval, we feel this search for meaning anew and afresh today, and perhaps wonder at the practicality or wisdom of looking to the past for insight or understanding into the good life.

And yet, the ancients remind us that "not even when one has an abundance does one's life consist of possessions"

(Luke 12:15). Abundant or meager as they may be, possessions must not make up the substance of one's life. Instead, their proper use necessarily involves right living in community. Perhaps the ancient Hebraic wisdom is particularly instructive in a time in which we might equate goodness with what we possess. "He has told you, *what is good*; and what does the Lord require of you but to do justice, to love kindness, and to walk humbly with your God?" (Micah 6:8) This vision of the good life, cast not when times were good, but during a time when calamity and exile awaited the nation of Israel offers an alternative understanding. Do justice, love kindness, and live out both of those virtues in light of humility before God; this is what is good and is the ground of the good life.

The wisdom of the ancients, from the Greeks and the Hebrews, suggests that the good life can be attained regardless of circumstance or possession. It shimmers in the wisdom of justice and kindness. It is found in the application of knowledge rightly applied in relationship to the world around us. It shines in humility before the God who is *good,* and is part and parcel of a relationship with that God. The good life is not bought or sold; it is not a prime real estate location, or a formula for success. The good life is our life offered to God and to others in justice, kindness, and humility.

Margaret Manning is a member of the speaking and writing team at Ravi Zacharias International Ministries in Seattle, Washington.

(1) A.L. Herman, *The Ways of Philosophy: Searching for a Worthwhile Life* (Scholars Press: Atlanta, 1990), 1.
(2) *Ibid*, 82.

*****

The article above gets to the heart of the heart of the matter quickly.

We are going to be discussing various ideas of the good life and then center on what exactly the good life is.

I need my readers to focus on the misconceptions of the good life and why they have become the so-called definitions of the good life.

One of my most favorite adages is this: "The best lie is often sandwiched between two truths." The good life as you know it is a lie and I will prove this to you.

Is the Good Life Unchanging Ideals—Justice, Truth, Goodness, Beauty?

In Chapter 1, my goal was to lay a good foundation to behavioral science and teach you how the human mind functions and why you do the things you do. The mechanism of the human mind is the same for both genders but the way each gender employs there psyche is different. There is no such thing as commercial versus personal mechanism of the mind. The human mind uses the same mechanism to make commercial decisions as well as personal decisions.

A good many of you would answer this question, "Is the Good Life Unchanging Ideals—Justice, Truth, Goodness, Beauty?" with a resounding "YES"! And you would be partially correct. The reason being is that your definition of justice, truth, goodness and beauty maybe skewed to the world's definition and not the correct definition.

Now take justice: recently as I write this the Boston Marathon bombers have been caught. The older brother was killed and the younger brother was wounded and captured. In the course that followed, a series of tweets and Facebook posts have sided with the younger brother based on a series of conspiracy theories that these brothers were set up. They ignore the fact that the younger brother in custody has admitted and confessed to the bombings and has stated in his affidavit that no other entity influenced him or his brother. Even with his admission and confession, the conspiracy theories abound and justice is skewed as these people backing these conspiracy theories line up demanding the younger brother's release.

Let's take truth: in today's world truth is defined subjectively or in other words, truth is anything you want it to be. Objective or absolute truth never changes and it is this truth I am speaking about here. But truth can hurt and sometimes it hurts enough causing people to make their own truths to rationalize some really weird behavior.

How about goodness: this is without a doubt the most skewed definition of them all. Goodness to most people is defined as favorable action towards others and this is true but goodness is more of a complete lifestyle rather than simply action.

The following article discusses both good and evil and really gives a fine perspective on both subjects....

Good and Evil
From Wikipedia, the free encyclopedia
http://en.wikipedia.org/wiki/Good_and_evil

In many religions, angels are considered good beings. In the Judeo-Christian tradition, God —being the creator of all life —is seen as the personification of good.

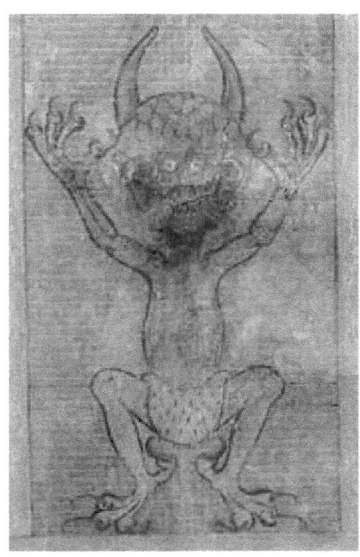

Satan, as seen in Codex Gigas. Demons are generally seen as evil beings and Satan as greatest of these (in the Christian tradition).

In religion, ethics, and philosophy, the dichotomy **"good and evil"** refers to the location on a linear spectrum of objects, desires, or behaviors, the *good* direction being morally positive, and the *evil* direction morally negative.

In cultures with Manichaean and Abrahamic religious influence, evil is usually perceived as the dualistic antagonistic opposite of good, in which good should prevail and evil should be defeated. In cultures with Buddhist spiritual influence, both good and evil are perceived as part of an antagonistic duality that itself must be overcome through achieving *Śūnyatā* meaning emptiness in the sense of recognition of good and evil

99

being two opposing principles but not a reality, emptying the duality of them, and achieving a oneness.

Origin of the concept

Every language has a word expressing *good* in the sense of "having the right or desirable quality" (ἀρετή) and *bad* in the sense "undesirable". A sense of moral judgement and a distinction "right and wrong, good and bad" are cultural universals.

Ancient world

In the eastern part of ancient Persia almost five thousand years ago a religious philosopher called Zoroaster simplified the pantheon of early Iranian gods into two opposing forces: Ahura Mazda (Illuminating Wisdom) and Angra Mainyu (Destructive Spirit) which were in conflict.

For the western world, this idea developed into a religion which spawned many sects, some of which embraced an extreme dualistic belief that the material world should be shunned and the spiritual world should be embraced. Gnostic ideas influenced many ancient religions which teach that *gnosis* (variously interpreted as enlightenment, salvation, emancipation or 'oneness with God') may be reached by practicing philanthropy to the point of personal poverty, sexual abstinence (as far as possible for *hearers*, total for *initiates*) and diligently searching for wisdom by helping others.

Classical world

In Western Civilization, the basic meanings of κακός and ἀγαθός are "bad, cowardly" and "good, brave, capable", and their absolute sense emerges only around 400 BC, with Pre-Socratic philosophy, in particular Democritus.

Morality in this absolute sense solidifies in the dialogues of Plato, together with the emergence of monotheistic thought (notably in *Euthyphro*, which ponders the concept of piety (τὸ ὅσιον) as a moral absolute). The idea is further developed in Late Antiquity by Neoplatonists, Gnostics, and Church Fathers.

This development from the relative or habitual to the absolute is also evident in the terms *ethics* and *morality* both being derived from terms for "regional custom", Greek ἠθος and Latin *mores*, respectively (see also *siðr*).

Medieval period

Medieval Christian philosophy was founded on the work of the Bishop Augustine of Hippo and theologian Thomas Aquinas who understood evil in terms of Biblical infallibility and Biblical inerrancy which they interpreted evil as the desire for anything remotely pleasurable to the human body.

Many medieval Christian theologians both broadened and narrowed the basic concept of *Good and evil* until it came to have several, sometimes complex definitions such as:

- a personal preference or subjective judgement regarding any issue which might be earn praise or punishment from the religious authorities

101

- religious obligation arising from Divine law leading to sainthood or damnation.
- a generally accepted cultural standard of behaviour which might enhance group survival or wealth
- natural law or behaviour which induces strong emotional reaction
- statute law imposing a legal duty

Modern Ideas

These basic ideas of a dichotomy have developed so that today:

- *Good* is a broad concept but it typically deals with an association with life, charity, continuity, happiness, love and justice.
- *Evil* is typically associated with conscious and deliberate wrongdoing, discrimination designed to harm others, humiliation of people designed to diminish their psychological needs and dignity, destructiveness, and acts of unnecessary and/or indiscriminate violence.
- the dilemma of the human condition and humans' and their capacity to perform both good and evil activities.

The nature of *being good* has been given many treatments; one is that the good is based on the natural love, bonding, and affection that begins at the earliest stages of personal development; another is that goodness is a product of knowing truth. Differing views also exist as to why evil might arise. Many religious and philosophical traditions claim that evil behavior is an *aberration* that results from the imperfect human condition (e.g. "The Fall of Man"). Sometimes, evil is attributed to the existence of free will and human agency. Some argue that evil itself is ultimately based in an ignorance of truth (i.e., human value, sanctity, divinity). A variety of Enlightenment thinkers have alleged the opposite, by suggesting that evil is learned as a consequence of tyrannical social structures.

Theories of moral goodness

Philosophers inquire into what sorts of things are good, and what the word "good" really means in the abstract. As a philosophical concept, goodness might represent a hope that natural love be *continuous, expansive,* and *all-inclusive.* In a monotheistic religious context, it is by this *hope* that an important concept of God is derived —as an infinite projection of love, manifest as goodness in the lives of people. In other contexts, the good is viewed to be whatever produces the best consequences upon the lives of people, especially with regard to their states of well being.

In religion, ethics, and philosophy, **goodness and evil**, or simply **good and evil**, refers to the concept of all human desires and behaviors as conforming to a *dualistic spectrum*—wherein in one direction are aspects that are *wisely reverent of life and continuity* ("good"), and in the other are aspects that are *vainly reverent of death and destruction* ("evil").

103

Religious and philosophical views tend to agree that, while "good and evil" is *a concept* and therefore *an abstraction*, **goodness** is intrinsic to human nature and is ultimately based on the natural love, bonding, affection that people grow to feel for other people. Likewise, most religious and philosophical interpretations agree that **evil** is ultimately based in an ignorance of truth (i.e. human value, sanctity, divinity), and evil behavior itself is an *aberration* —one that defies any understanding save that the path to evil is one of confusion and excessive desire (greed). In physics and statistical thermodynamics, the property of goodness or order is often referred to as a state of low entropy.

As a philosophical abstraction, goodness represents a hope that natural love be *continuous, expansive,* and *all-inclusive.* In religious context, it is by this *hope* that an important concept of God is derived —as an infinite projection of love, manifest as goodness in the lives of people. The belief in such hope is often translated as "faith", and wisdom itself is largely defined within religious doctrine as *a knowledge and understanding of innate goodness.* The concepts of innocence, spiritual purity, and salvation are likewise related to a concept of being in, or returning to, a state of *goodness*—one that, according to various teachings of "enlightenment", approaches a state of *holiness* (or Godliness*).*

Descriptive, meta-ethical, and normative fields

It is possible to treat the essential theories of value by the use of a philosophical and academic approach. In properly analyzing theories of value, everyday beliefs are

104

not only carefully *catalogued* and *described*, but also rigorously *analyzed* and *judged*.

There are at least two basic ways of presenting a theory of value, based on two different kinds of questions:

- What do people find good, and what do they despise?
- What really is good, and what really is bad?

The two questions are subtly different. One may answer the first question by researching the world by use of social science, and examining the preferences that people assert. However, one may answer the second question by use of reasoning, introspection, prescription, and generalization.

The former kind of method of analysis is called "descriptive", because it attempts to describe what people actually view as good or evil; while the latter is called "normative", because it tries to actively prohibit evils and cherish goods. These descriptive and normative approaches can be complementary. For example, tracking the decline of the popularity of slavery across cultures is the work of descriptive ethics, while advising that slavery be avoided is normative.

Meta-ethics is the study of the fundamental questions concerning the nature and origins of the good and the evil, including inquiry into the nature of good and evil, as well as the meaning of evaluative language. In this respect, meta-ethics is not necessarily tied to investigations into how others see the good, or of asserting what is good.

Theories of the intrinsically good

A satisfying formulation of goodness is valuable because it might allow one to construct a good life or society by reliable processes of deduction, elaboration, or prioritization. One could answer the ancient question, "How should we then live?" among many other important related questions. It has long been thought that this question can best be answered by examining what it is that necessarily makes a thing valuable, or in what the source of value consists.

Transcendental realism

One attempt to define goodness describes it as a property of the world. According to this claim, to talk about the good is to talk about something real that exists in the object itself, independent of the perception of it. Plato advocated this view, in his expression that there is such a thing as an eternal realm of forms or ideas, and that the greatest of the ideas and the essence of being was goodness, or The good.

The good was defined by many ancient Greeks and other ancient philosophers as a perfect and eternal idea, or blueprint. The good is the right relation between all that exists, and this exists in the mind of the Divine, or some heavenly realm. The good is the harmony of a just political community, love, friendship, the ordered human soul of virtues, and the right relation to the Divine and to

Nature. The characters in Plato's dialogues mention the many virtues of a philosopher, or a lover of wisdom.

A theist is a person who believes that gods exist (monotheism or polytheism). A theist may, therefore, claim that the universe has a purpose and value according to the will of such creator(s) that lies partially beyond human understanding. For instance, Thomas Aquinas—a proponent of this view—believed he had proven the existence of God, and the right relations that humans ought to have to the divine first cause.

Monotheists might also hope for infinite universal love. Such hope is often translated as "faith", and wisdom itself is largely defined within some religious doctrines as *a knowledge and understanding of innate goodness.*

The concepts of innocence, spiritual purity, and salvation are likewise related to a concept of being in, or returning to, a state of *goodness*—one that, according to various teachings of "enlightenment", approaches a state of *holiness* (or Godliness). A dystheist or atheist, however, may potentially believe that the concept of goodness is not related to deities.

Perfectionism

Aristotle believed that virtues consisted of realization of potentials unique to humanity, such as the use of reason. This type of view, called perfectionism, has been recently defended in modern form by Thomas Hurka.

An entirely different form of perfectionism has arisen in response to rapid technological change. Some techno-optimists, especially transhumanists, avow a form of perfectionism in which the capacity to determine good and trade off fundamental values, is expressed not by humans but by software, genetic engineering of humans, artificial intelligence.

Skeptics assert that rather than perfect goodness, it would be only the appearance of perfect goodness, reinforced by persuasion technology and probably brute force of violent technological escalation, which would cause people to accept such rulers or rules authored by them.

Welfarist theories

Welfarist theories of value say things that are good are such because of their positive effects on human well-being.

Subjective theories of wellbeing

It is difficult to figure out where an immaterial trait such as "goodness" could reside in the world. A counterproposal is to locate values inside people. Some philosophers go so far as to say that if some state of affairs does not tend to arouse a desirable subjective state in self-aware beings, then it cannot be good.

Most philosophers that think goods have to create desirable mental states also say that goods are experiences of self-aware beings. These philosophers often distinguish the experience, which they call an intrinsic good, from the things that seem to cause the experience, which they call "inherent" goods. Failing to distinguish the two leads to a subject-object problem in which it is not clear who is evaluating what object.

Some theories describe no higher collective value than that of maximizing *pleasure* for individual(s). Some even define goodness and intrinsic value as the experience of pleasure, and bad as the experience of pain. This view is called hedonism, a *monistic theory of value*. It has two main varieties: simple, and Epicurean.

Simple hedonism is the view that physical pleasure is the ultimate good. However, the ancient philosopher Epicurus used the word 'pleasure' in a more general sense that encompassed a range of states from bliss to contentment to relief. Contrary to popular caricature, he valued pleasures of the mind to bodily pleasures, and advocated moderation as the surest path to happiness.

Jeremy Bentham's book *The Principles of Morals and Legislation* prioritized goods by considering pleasure, pain and consequences. This theory had a wide effect on public affairs, up to and including the present day. A similar system was later named Utilitarianism by John Stuart Mill. More broadly, utilitarian theories are examples of Consequentialism. All utilitarian theories are based upon the *maxim of utility*, which states that *good* is whatever provides *the greatest happiness for the greatest number*. It follows from this principle that what brings happiness to the greatest number of people is good.

A benefit of tracing good to pleasure and pain is that both are easily understandable, both in oneself and to an extent in others. For the hedonist, the explanation for helping behaviour may come in the form of *empathy*—the ability of a being to "feel" another's pain. People tend to value the lives of gorillas more than those of mosquitoes because the gorilla lives and feels, making it easier to empathize with them. This idea is carried forward in the ethical relationship view and has given rise to the animal rights movement and parts of the peace movement. The impact of sympathy on human behaviour is compatible with Enlightenment views, including David Hume's stances that the idea of a self with unique identity is illusory, and that morality ultimately comes down to sympathy and fellow feeling for others, or the exercise of approval underlying moral judgments.

A view adopted by James Griffin attempts to find a subjective alternative to hedonism as an intrinsic value. He argues that the satisfaction of one's informed desires constitutes well-being, whether or not these desires actually bring the agent happiness. Moreover, these preferences must be life-relevant, that is, contribute to the success of a person's life overall.

Desire satisfaction may occur without the agent's awareness of the satisfaction of the desire. For example, if a man wishes for his legal will to be enacted after his death, and it is, then his desire has been satisfied even though he will never experience or know of it.

Objective theories of wellbeing

The idea that the ultimate good exists and is not orderable but is globally measurable is reflected in various ways in economic (classical economics, green economics, welfare economics, Gross National Happiness) and scientific (positive psychology, the Science of morality) well-being measuring theories, all of which focus on various ways of assessing progress towards that goal, a so-called Genuine Progress Indicator. Modern economics thus reflects very ancient philosophy, but a calculation or quantitative or other process based on cardinality and statistics replaces the simple ordering of values.

For example, in both economics and in folk wisdom, the value of something seems to rise so long as it is relatively scarce. However, if it becomes too scarce, it leads often to a conflict, and can reduce collective value.

In the classical political economy of Adam Smith and David Ricardo, and in its critique by Karl Marx, *human labor* is seen as the ultimate source of all new economic value. This is an *objective* theory of value (see value theory), which attributes value to real production-costs, and ultimately expenditures of human labor-time (see also law of value).

It contrasts with marginal utility theory, which argues that the value of labor depends on subjective preferences by consumers, which may however also be objectively studied.

The economic value of labor may be assessed technically in terms of its use-value or utility or commercially in terms of its exchange-value, price or production cost (see also labor power. But its value may also be socially assessed in terms of its contribution to the wealth and well-being of a society.

In non-market societies, labor may be valued primarily in terms of skill, time, and output, as well as moral or social criteria and legal obligations. In market societies, labor is valued economically primarily through the labor market.

The price of labor may then be set by supply and demand, by strike action or legislation, or by legal or professional entry-requirements into occupations.

Mid-range theories

Conceptual metaphor theories argue against both subjective and objective conceptions of value and meaning, and focus on the relationships between body and other essential elements of human life. In effect, conceptual metaphor theories treat ethics as an ontology problem and the issue of how to work-out values as a negotiation of these metaphors, not the application of some abstraction or a strict standoff between parties who have no way to understand each other's views.

Goodness and agency
Agent-centered theories

One more recent philosophical proposal has defined good as "That which increases the quality and quantity of choices available overall." These approaches have been called *choice optimization theories*. This maxim might be countered by the phenomenon of opportunity costs observed by social scientists. Opportunity cost is when people who are confronted with a greater number of choices also experience greater dismay at their choices after the fact, because of the missed opportunities.

In his *Development as Freedom*, Amartya Sen asserted free time as the most fundamental good, and systems of organizing that enabled it as the most fundamental value in civilization. He refuted the common claim that Asian value theorists had devalued freedom and was clear that a marketplace (creating unity via pricing) valuing free time could be created. Marilyn Waring took a similar view from a feminist perspective, arguing women's time was undervalued and especially the free time they used to raise and teach children. Waring also strongly denied that military hardware or activities were of any value, and attempted to reconcile peace or welfare views of good with the ecological values.

Other agent-centered theories amongst contemporary thinkers such as Bernard Williams seek to revive the old concept (associated for example with Aristotle and Confucius, that the right action is the action that a person of good character (the "great-souled man" as Aristotle said) will perform.

Goodwill

John Rawls' book *A Theory of Justice* prioritized social arrangements and goods based on their contribution to justice. Rawls defined justice as *fairness*, especially in distributing social goods, defined fairness in terms of procedures, and attempted to prove that just institutions and lives are good, if rational individuals' goods are considered fairly. Rawls's crucial invention was the original position, a procedure in which one tries to make objective moral decisions by refusing to let personal facts about oneself enter one's moral calculations.

One problem with the thinkings of Rawls is that it is overly procedural. Procedurally fair processes of the type used by Rawls may not leave enough room for judgment, and therefore, reduce the totality of goodness. For example, if two people are found to own an orange, the standard fair procedure is to cut it in two and give half to each. However, if one wants to eat it while the other wants the rind to flavor a cake, cutting it in two is clearly less good than giving the peel to the baker and feeding the core to the eater.

Applying procedural fairness to an entire society therefore seems certain to create recognizable inefficiencies and therefore be unfair, and (by the equivalence of justice with fairness) unjust.

However, procedural processes are not always necessarily damning in this way. Immanuel Kant, a great influence for Rawls, similarly applies a lot of procedural practice within the practical application of *The Categorical Imperative*; however, this is indeed not based solely on 'fairness'. Even though an example like the one above regarding the orange would not be something that required the practical application of *The Categorical Imperative*, it is important to draw distinction between Kant and Rawls, and note that Kant's Theory would not necessarily lead to the same problems Rawls' does — i.e., the cutting in half of the orange. Kant's Theory promotes acting out of Duty — acting for the Summum Bonum for him, *The Good Will* - and in fact encourages Judgement, too. What this would mean is that the outcome of the Orange's distribution would not be such a simple process for Kant as the reason why it would be wanted by both parties would necessarily have to be a part of the Judgement process, thus eliminating the problem that Rawls' account suffers here.

Agent-external theories
Society, life and ecology

Many views value *unity* as a good: to go beyond eudaimonia by saying that an individual person's flourishing is valuable only as a means to the flourishing of society as a whole. In other words, a single person's life is, ultimately, not important or worthwhile in itself, but is good only as a means to the success of society as a whole. Some elements of Confucianism are an example of this, encouraging the view that people ought to conform as individuals to demands of a peaceful and ordered society.

According to the naturalistic view, the flourishing of society is not, or not the only, intrinsically good thing. Defenses of this notion are often formulated by reference to biology, and observations that living things compete more with their own kind than with other kinds. Rather, what is of intrinsic good is the flourishing of all sentient life, extending to those animals that have some level of similar sentience, such as Great Ape personhood. Others go farther, declaring that life itself is of intrinsic value.

115

By another approach, one achieves peace and agreement by focusing, not on one's peers (who may be rivals or competitors), but on the common environment. The reasoning: As living beings it is clearly and objectively good that we are surrounded by an ecosystem that supports life. Indeed, if we weren't, we could neither discuss that good nor even recognize it. The anthropic principle in cosmology recognizes this view.

Under materialism or even embodiment values, or in any system that recognizes the validity of ecology as a scientific study of limits and potentials, an ecosystem is a fundamental good. To all who investigate, it seems that goodness, or value, exists within an ecosystem, Earth. Creatures within that ecosystem and wholly dependent on it, evaluate good relative to what else could be achieved there. In other words, good is situated in a particular place and one does not dismiss everything that is not available there (such as very low gravity or absolutely abundant sugar candy) as "not good enough", one works within its constraints. Transcending them and learning to be satisfied with them, is thus another sort of value, perhaps called satisfaction, or in Buddhism, enlightenment.

Values and the people that hold them seem necessarily subordinate to the ecosystem. If this is so, then what kind of being could validly apply the word "good" to an ecosystem as a whole? Who would have the power to assess and judge an ecosystem as good or bad? By what criteria? And by what criteria would ecosystems be modified, especially larger ones such as the atmosphere (climate change) or oceans (extinction) or forests (deforestation)?

"Remaining on Earth" as the most basic value. While green ethicists have been most forthright about it, and have developed theories of Gaia philosophy, biophilia, bioregionalism that reflect it, the questions are now universally recognized as central in determining value, e.g. the economic "value of Earth" to humans as a whole, or the "value of life" that is neither whole-Earth nor human. Many have come to the conclusion that without assuming ecosystem continuation as a universal good, with attendant virtues like biodiversity and ecological wisdom it is impossible to justify such operational requirements as sustainability of human activity on Earth.

One response is that humans are not necessarily confined to Earth, and could use it and move on. A counter-argument is that only a tiny fraction of humans could do this—and they would be self-selected by ability to do technological escalation on others (for instance, the ability to create large spacecraft to flee the planet in, and simultaneously fend off others who seek to prevent them). Another counter-argument is that extraterrestrial life would encounter the fleeing humans and destroy them as a locust species. A third is that if there are no other worlds fit to support life (and no extraterrestrials who compete with humans to occupy them) it is both futile to flee, and foolish to imagine that it would take less energy and skill to protect the Earth as a habitat than it would take to construct some new habitat.

Accordingly remaining on Earth, as a living being surrounded by a working ecosystem, is a fair statement of the most basic values and goodness to any being we are able to communicate with. A moral system without this axiom seems simply not actionable.

However, most religious systems acknowledge an afterlife and improving this is seen as an even more basic good. In many other moral systems, also, remaining on Earth in a state that lacks honor or power over self is less desirable — consider seppuku in bushido, kamikazes or the role of suicide attacks in Jihadi rhetoric. In all these systems, remaining on Earth is perhaps no higher than a third-place value.

Radical values environmentalism can be seen as either a very old or a very new view: that the only intrinsically good thing is a flourishing ecosystem; individuals and societies are merely instrumentally valuable, good only as means to having a flourishing ecosystem. The Gaia philosophy is the most detailed expression of this overall thought but it strongly influenced Deep Ecology and the modern Green Parties.

It is often claimed that aboriginal peoples never lost this sort of view. Anthropological linguistics studies links between their languages and the ecosystems they lived in, which gave rise to their knowledge distinctions. Very often, environmental cognition and moral cognition were not distinguished in these languages. Offenses to nature were like those to other people, and Animism reinforced this by giving nature "personality" via myth.

Anthropological theories of value explore these questions.

Most people in the world reject older situated ethics and localized religious views. However small-community-based and ecology-centric views have gained some popularity in recent years. In part, this has been attributed to the desire for ethical certainties. Such a deeply rooted definition of goodness would be valuable because it might allow one to construct a good life or society by reliable processes of deduction, elaboration or prioritization. Ones that relied only on local referents one could verify for oneself, creating more certainty and therefore less investment in protection, hedging and insuring against consequences of loss of the value.

History and novelty

An event is often seen as being of value simply because of its *novelty* in fashion and art. By contrast, cultural history and other antiques are sometimes seen as of value in and of themselves due to their *age*. Philosopher-historians Will and Ariel Durant spoke as much with the quote, "As the sanity of the individual lies in the continuity of his memories, so the sanity of the group lies in the continuity of its traditions; in either case a break in the chain invites a neurotic reaction" (The Lessons of History, 72).

Assessment of the value of old or historical artifacts takes into consideration, especially but not exclusively: the value placed on having a detailed knowledge of the past, the desire to have tangible ties to ancestral history, and/or the increased market value scarce items traditionally hold.

Creativity and innovation and invention are sometimes upheld as fundamentally good especially in Western industrial society — all imply newness, and even opportunity to profit from novelty. Bertrand Russell was notably pessimistic about creativity and thought that knowledge expanding faster than wisdom necessarily was fatal.

Goodness and morality in biology

The issue of good and evil in the human makeup, often associated with morality, is regarded by some biologists (notably Edward O. Wilson, Jeremy Griffith, David Sloan Wilson and Frans de Waal) as an important question to be addressed by the field of biology.

*****

The ancient Geeks viewed goodness and beauty as paramount to the foundational base of their society. There is a saying, "The grandeur that was Greece and the glory that was Rome," and this is basically true.

The ancient Greeks had a tremendously "skewed' view of the world. On their battle shields they emblazoned symbols of peace on weapons of war. Their ideals did not match their actions and their quest or empire proved this fact.

Any moral act, whether good or bad is defined by action and not just by words. There is a bible story that describes this fact:

"But what do you think? A man had two sons. He went to the first and said, 'Son, go and work in the vineyard today.' His son replied, 'I don't want to,' but later he changed his mind and went. Then the father went to the other son and told him the same thing. He replied, 'I will, sir,' but he didn't go. Which of the two did the father's will?" They answered, "The first." Jesus said to them, "Truly I tell you, tax collectors and prostitutes will get into God's kingdom ahead of you. Matthew 21: 28-31

Action speaks louder than words!!!

Chapter 2 – Online Body Language

In this section I am going to teach you how to identify and profile a con man. First, I am going to show you how to spot a con man in the "physical world, and then I will teach you how to spot a con man in the "cyber-world" using "Social Media Body Language".

How to Spot a Con Man in the Physical World

Secrets, lies and tricks are tactics many con artists use to manipulate people to get what they want, oftentimes destroying their victim's lives forever. Con artists gain a person's confidence so they can have easy access to the victim's money, trust and friendship. To avoid being fooled by a con artists look out for the following warning signs:

Blending In
Effective con artists must disguise their true motives. They try hard to look and talk like others in the community and quickly get to know a lot of people.

Talking the Talk
Con artists learn vocabulary so they sound knowledgeable in the subject they are talking about.

Dressing for Success
Con artists want others to believe that they are regular folks, but they work hard to come across as smooth, professional and successful.

Bringing out the Worst in You

123

Con artists often expose your negative traits such as greed, fear and insecurity. They know that big promises with no risk get people's attention. They also try and make you feel inadequate if you don't believe what they are telling you, or are asking too many questions.

Fair-Weather Friends
At the beginning, con artists are very friendly and take a personal interest in you. After they get what they want, con artists minimize their contact with you.

Moving Frequently
Even the best con artists can only play the part for so long before people become suspicious of their behaviors and motives.

To ensure that you never fall victim to the scam of a con artist, don't trust a person too easily. Always do your homework and investigate a person and the claims he/she is making before giving him/her your money or signing a contract. If you fear you may be dealing with a con, stop speaking with the person and do not give him/her any personal information.

Red Flags

If you've already entered into a transaction with someone, keep an eye out for the following warning signs:

- Secrecy - Are you asked not to tell anyone?
- Cash only - Many (but not all) con artists don't like to be paid by check because it leaves a paper trail.

- Jackpot just around the corner - The con artist is stringing you along while he or she collects more money from you (e.g. "Any day now...). Your own denial might allow this procrastination to go on far longer than common sense would allow, because you don't want to face the possibility that you've been duped.
- Procrastination turns into intimidation - When your patience runs thin and you begin to question the con artist's credibility, you may end up getting treated like a traitor, or even a fool. They might try to intimidate you so you'll stick around until they can flee with the money. (E.g. "You're as guilty as I am in this.")

Know Your Own Weaknesses

These are the characteristics and situations that con artists most often exploit:

- Loneliness
- Sense of charity
- Desperation regarding money (e.g. heavily indebted, business financial problems)
- Being unhappy with your life, and a tendency to look for a "quick fix"
- Falling in love (If a new romantic interest wants you to throw in your lot with theirs, get a second opinion! Ask your family and professionals for their advice.)

Common Scams

- Home improvement - repairs or improvements you don't need
- Bank - false bank examiner; the con artist asks the victim (usually an older widow) to test the honesty of employees by withdrawing substantial funds, which are given to the con artist for "examination". The victim is given a fake receipt and the con artist disappears with the cash.
- Investment - franchises, vending machines, land frauds, theft of inventions, securities investments, work-at-home
- Postal frauds - chain letters, magazine subscriptions, unordered merchandise, correspondence courses
- Others: bait and switch, charity rackets, computer dating, debt consolidation, contracts, dance lessons, freezer plans, psychic fraud, fortune tellers, health clubs, job placement, lonely hearts, medical quackery, missing heirs, referral sales, talent scouts, pyramid schemes, fake officials.

Sociopaths use flattery and inflated credentials. They talk fast, pushing you for fast decisions. Sooner or later, you will have a run-in with a sociopath. There are just too many of them—possibly between 3 million and 12 million sociopaths in America. And they aren't necessarily locked up in jail. Sociopaths roam through all parts of society, all areas of the country, all walks of life.

There is only one way to protect yourself from sociopaths: You must know what they are, and put your guard up when you start seeing the symptoms.

Sociopaths are prolific con artists. Here are some typical con artist tricks.

Lavish flattery

If you've just met someone who is overwhelming you with praise, attention and concern, be careful. Be particularly careful if you're lonely and looking for love—con artists know exactly how to play that tune.

Credentials—exaggerated and fabricated

Con artists may "prove" themselves by namedropping or volunteering detailed resumes or credentials. If you're at all suspicious, check their references.

Building your trust

Con artists will sometimes honor their commitments in the beginning so that you begin to trust them. They'll pay back initial loans, or appear to be unselfishly helping other people. Their objective is to get you to drop your guard.

The story doesn't quite add up

The con artist's story may have small inconsistencies or unexplained loose ends. If you ask questions, the con will glibly provide an explanation—which may also not add up. Or, he or she will sidestep the issue by accusing you of paranoia or mistrust.

"I need an answer now."

A crisis needs to be averted, an opportunity will disappear—whatever the reason, a con artist will want an answer right away. If you have time to think, research or ask advice, you may realize that con artist's plan is a ploy. The con will want your money before you figure it out.

Intense eye contact

Typically, when people talk to each other, they look each other in the eyes and then briefly look away. Sociopathic con artists often exhibit a "predatory stare"—unblinking, fixated and emotionless. It's not a sign of empathy—it's an effort to assert control.

Isolation

Con artists will slowly and subtly separate you from people who may question their plans. They may intercept phone calls from your friends. They may refuse to associate with your family. They'll tell you, "It's you and me against the world, baby." Soon, you're alone with them, snared in their net.

How to Spot a Con Man in the Cyber-World

In this section, I want to teach you the differences in gender words and how the male and female psyches differ on a variety of subjects. I will be taking information from the research files at Applied Mind Sciences. Once you learn the difference in how men and women write content and communicate, you will be able to spot the people posing as the opposite gender.

*****

Regarding men: A man thinks in progressive steps...
In the male psyche, progressive thought is tied to objective reasoning. Men are task oriented. Because of this, their progressive thought, and objective reasoning, is due to the fact that men need to assign tasks. This is the underlying foundation to a man's existence. Task orientation is very important in men. Priorities are assigned and solutions are accomplished, in an orderly fashion. Men appear to have retained the original spiritual characteristic of employing their intellects first, but almost always, express everything in the physical. Do not become confused into believing that men are more spiritual than women are. Actually, the opposite is true; women are more spiritual than men are. Men employ their intellects, more so, than women do, but only in the fact, they use it as a filter, and express through the physical. Women filter most of the stimuli that comes to them, through their emotions, but do not have any problem employing their intellects as filters to their expression. As taught previously, women filter stimuli using emotions, physical, spiritual, and intellect, and are quite comfortable within all for traits. Men, however, are only comfortable within the intellect and physical traits. Men use their emotions as relief valves, while women view emotions as warning signs. In other words, women use emotions as filter to expression, and men completely avoid emotions as filters, using them simply as expressions of relief.

Women are more finely attuned to their inner existences. They view change as a necessity, where men are highly resistant to change. With the male/female orientation of single parent homes, that I spoke about earlier, change is, and in most cases, now a very big reality in male/female psyches. I, personally, know quite a few women who live and die for football. This androgynous behavior is becoming more and more of a reality between the genders, and women find this easy to accomplish, where men are highly resistant. Have you noticed that men view women as invading their turf, when it comes to clubs, where they have exclusive male memberships only? Women will dress in men's clothing, but men do not wear female attire? These are only but a few examples where women are comfortable with change, but even this has its drawbacks. Women constantly view men strictly from within their own framework of expression. Women cannot seem to understand why men cannot view the world as they do, or see things as they see them. Men can do this if they are taught, but they are resistant to change. People, who claim they cannot change, are wrong. This is a "cop-out" and a sad commentary to a person's character. To a man, a need to change must be demonstrated. To a woman, change is a given.

Men externalize everything; women internalize everything. Men view courtship as a task; women refuse to accept this premise because, to them, it implies a process they feel should be more emotional, rather than task oriented. I am sure you have heard women who lament the fact that their mates treat them as objects. More often than not, this is true. But it is almost never meant in a demeaning sense, as most women misinterpret it to be. A man is object-oriented, but what draws a man

130

to a woman is the mystery, which surrounds her. Is a man wrong for thinking in this objective way? Absolutely not! Unless their objectivity takes on a demeaning quality, this is the how a man employs his psyche. For example, a man who simply views a woman, as an object of sexual gratification, is emphatically wrong, but a man who views his wife, as his possession is not.

A man does not consciously understand his objective nature. This is just the way he is, and in his mind, he is not being cruel or demeaning. A man may view his wife as his property, in the sense of possession, but this trait stems from a man's need for boundaries, and his inherent nature to provide protection. History tells us that cities, in ancient times, had walls built around them for protection. Subconsciously, men continue to build walls around what they hold dear, as a symbol of protection. Culture plays a very big role in this male trait of objective orientation. Some cultures actually view women as chattel. I am presently counseling a woman who was married to an Arab. When she converted to Christianity, he threw her out and divorced her. She has four small children, and needless to say, the whole sordid affair has had its toll on them, as well as the woman. In this case, culture exercises a wrongful reaction. Where is the love? Where are the compassion and the understanding of responsibility, on the father's part?

Conversely, here in America, women are entering the workplace in increasing numbers. They are demanding to be treated, in pay, benefits, recognition, and perks, the same as their male counterparts...and rightly so. However, through the feminist movement, women have used coercion and threats to seek this "sameness." Men understand confrontation. It is a very big part of the male

131

psyche. Women abhor confrontation. Fighting with a man is bringing the battle to his territory, and in a format, he understands. This is plain dumb! When a woman begins to understand the male psyche, and the steps a man employs, in bringing about change, then, and only then, will they find that which they seek. How to men change? The same way they think: PROGRESSIVELY!

Let's talk about the way men change. Men are not open to change. Women, on the other hand, cannot conceive of life without change. It is easy to see why conflict can develop, until you understand how both genders view change. Men view change as upsetting the status quo. "If it ain't broke, don't fix it," is their battle cry. Change, to a man, comes about due to an intellectual decision, and is very rarely an emotional reaction. Change is employed gradually, since a man needs to be constantly evaluating his surroundings. Spontaneity is a rare quality in a man because this implies frivolous behavior. Men view change as requiring energy to accomplish, and men are always subconsciously evaluating their actions, based on energy expenditure.

Women, on the other hand, view change as a direct response to experiencing life. Because they operate on a multi-level plane, of being able to think and experience many things at once, change is necessary, since it is the effect of experience, and its requirement to alter one's actions due, to the discovery of something better. This is important: <u>change, to a woman, is always associated with the betterment of something.</u> A woman expects her man to change, for the better, as they grow within their relationship. Women view this growth as a natural progression in life. Men do not! I use the example, quite often, of the movie "As Good As It Gets," with Jack

Nicholson and Helen Hunt. In this movie, Nicholson's character makes the statement, "She makes me want to be a better man." To a woman, this defines her man, and even though I hate it when Hollywood gets it right, they got it really right here! A man in love with a woman will want to be a better man for her, and the woman actually causes this to happen by love. In other words, coercion rarely works with men; change occurs because men want to change. Wanting to change is very different from needing to change. Men change progressively, after they have determined change is necessary. Women can cause this change by progressively allowing the man to see that change is necessary, and a good thing. Let me give you an example:

A husband and wife, who had been married for eight years, and had three small children, came to me for counseling. The husband was an attorney; the wife did not work outside the home. The wife complained that her husband, when he came home in the evening, would plop himself down in his easy chair and watch television. She would make dinner, clean up, and watch the children. He would not ask to help her, and when she wanted to go out in the evening, to socialize with her girlfriends, he would complain about watching the children. She also complained that he never wanted to talk with her. Does all of this sound familiar?

Let's look at this situation from an intellectual standpoint. We can all easily see the emotional response here. Remember, men have a lower energy level than women; hence, when the husband came home from work, he was exhausted and weary from the mental, as well as the physical, demands of his profession. By allowing the man to rest and recharge his batteries, for a couple of hours, the wife would be able to enlist the husband's help in watching the children, engaging him in conversation, and helping with some of the household chores. Now, many of you would say that the wife was doing all of the sacrificing, but that is an emotional response. In my last book, I taught that love is sacrifice not compromise. I have also taught that doing your best is not always good enough; sometimes you must do what is required. Read on...

The husband can readily be taught that the wife has needs, which must be met. He can intellectually, understand the wife's need to get away from the children; have some time to interact with her girlfriends, and the fact that he should help her with the household chores. By allowing him to rest, when he came home, his energy level increased. By progressively taking each task, one at a time, he could begin to watch the children, then help out, and then engage his wife in conversation. To attempt to do this all at once would not be successful. Change must be progressive. When the wife took my advice and progressively introduced change, her husband responded to watching the children very enthusiastically. He began to enjoy his mentoring role and looked forward to the time when she would go and visit her girlfriends. Of course, upon her return, the house looked like a cyclone had hit it but, hey, I am only a psychologist; I am not God!

He also readily embraced the idea of the need to talk to his wife, and they both decided to hold family meetings. They even included the children in this function, which was very smart. The need to help around the house is going to take a little more time but both the wife and I are PROGRESSIVELY working on it.

The important thing in this example was the wife's understanding of her husband's psyche. Once she understood how her husband employed his psyche, she now had the tools to make her marriage BETTER! Conversely, the husband had to be taught the way his wife employed her psyche. He easily understood his wife's need for change and experience. Part of that experiencing is conversation. He did not embrace the idea of helping with the chores but once again, culture played a role in his mindset. He grew up in a culture where women did all the housework. This will take some time and education, but I am confident he will see his wife's need in this since it is obvious he loves her dearly. Let's continue...

Progressive thought consumes a man's psyche. Women constantly accuse men of being anal, in their approach to life, but this is simply not true. The act of being anal implies that change is impossible. Men are very capable of change. A woman who enters a relationship with a man demanding change is in for a rude awakening. Men are not so easily coerced or cajoled into change. Change requires a reason in men, not in women. If you go to close a door with a foot in it, either you can force the door closed with the foot still in it or you can remove the foot. From my standpoint, it is easier to remove the foot. In other words, it is easier to demonstrate a need to change rather than to force it.

This leads to one of my premises, in my last book, which was vehemently attacked; specifically compromise versus sacrifice. My premise was to never compromise but to always sacrifice. Men understand sacrifice very well. They give up many things to acquire other things, which in their minds are better. Sacrifice is an intellectual

135

decision; compromise is an emotional decision. Compromise, on the other hand, is not an easy concept for men. It implies giving up more than they receive back, and this causes resentment. Plus, compromise, to a man, is a result of coercion or cajolery. Men resist both of these acts.

A man's mind is linear, and this means he goes to Step A, and when this is finished, he proceeds to Step B, etc.

As I stated above, a man's psyche employs linear and progressive reasoning, to everything that confronts him. He has an inherent need to assign tasks. Solutions, to these tasks, are also derived in a progressive manner, but utilize intellectual thought, rather than emotional rationalization. Women misunderstand this need in a man, and constantly label men as being stubborn, insensitive, etc. Women, who make a conscious decision to constantly fight with a man, find out very quickly that a man will happily engage them in battle. A man's response to confrontation is highly dependent on the maturity level of the man, both emotionally and intellectually.

My wife would get upset with me whenever I made decisions that she felt we should have made together. It would have been very easy to respond arrogantly that, as head of the family, it was my domain to make the decisions, but this would have been an immature response. It is an immature response because it hides behind ego, stupidity, and apathy. My wife had every right to be involved in the family decisions. She was the other part that made up the whole, of our oneness, in marriage. Instead of getting upset, I would listen and then

136

give her a hug and a kiss, and include her in everything I could think of. By so doing, not only did I not have to sleep on the couch, with the dog *(remember him from my last book?),* but I also didn't have to see my wife upset. Besides, she was very good at finances and organization, and with her help, we not only became a better team but it gave us many things to do together and converse about.

Men, because they operate on a physical plain more so than women, have a tendency to use violence and physical confrontation more than a woman. This is also an immature response, where men have been trained to acquire what they want through coercion and violence. Anger management plays a big factor here. Violent people can control their anger, but choose to use it as a tool to get what they want, and almost always express it in the physical. There are many physical causes to anger, too many to begin an in depth discussion here. It is not always a wrongful choice. A physical malady may be the culprit, and in treatment, I always require a medical physical first.

A man's linear mind is also a result of his need for security and boundaries. Everything has a proper place, for a man, and his progressive thought patterns allow him to check off needed items, or tasks, requiring attention. Men choose to compartmentalize their existences. Love is not an exception to the rule here either. Women misunderstand a man's need for boundaries and compartmentalization, because there is nothing to compare this with in their psyches. Spontaneity requires a man to come outside this compartmentalization, and this is difficult for a man...but not impossible. Men spend a good deal of their lives within their minds. Men find it difficult to live within their emotions because social mores are against this type of behavior. Emotions, hence, are most always expressed in the physical. Women misinterpret this trait as not being emotional. Physical expressions of emotions are warning signals to women, and so when a man does express emotions physically, women have a tendency to become anxious and nervous. In other words, they misunderstand a man's need to release stress and anxiety, using physical expression. How many of you women simply cannot understand your mate's need to watch sports and carry on as little boys, punching and shoving each other as the game progresses? Sports are a physical release, not only in the actual playing of the game but also in observation of the game. Women do not see this fact and within their psyches, it is alien and strange. Women act out their stress and anxiety by talking to one another and sharing experiences. Men view this as an exercise in futility. Social conversation between men is very different than it is between women. You only have to eavesdrop on each genders conversation to see this difference.

My wife would spend the day shopping with her girlfriends and then come home and be on the phone with them talking for another couple of hours. Why? She had just spent the day with them. How much is there to talk about? However, it wasn't just the talking that was happening. My wife and her girlfriends were sharing experiences, working out the stresses in their own lives, and interacting with one another. Women spend a good deal of time talking about their men to one another. Men rarely talk about their wives to one another unless something is wrong and then sometimes you have to pull it out of them.

A man is object oriented and his progressive nature enables him to assign tasks.

We have discussed this subject in detail. The task assigning nature of a man is important in the way a man conduct's his life. Unlike a woman, a man is not capable of multiple thought function, and subjective reasoning, unless the man is purposely trained to function in this manner. A man finds a need to assign tasks based on energy outlay, priority, and benefit. Since a woman, by nature, has more body fat than a man does, she also has a higher energy level. Men subconsciously evaluate everything according to energy outlay. When a man comes home from work and is tired, a woman would be wise to let him rest for an hour, and then say to him, "Let's go to the movies." Once a man has recharged his batteries, he will be more responsive to a woman's need to experience things. This is important in conversation too. Women are expressing animals, and this expression finds its outlet in conversation. Men, by nature, are not expressing animals, insofar as conversation is concerned. They are more expressive in a physical way. By allowing a man to rest, he becomes more attuned to his wife's need to converse.

I want to point out a very important thing to all of my reading audience. If allowed to rest and recharge his batteries, it is my premise that, a man will become more responsive to the female. NEVERTHELESS, all of you have had experiences where this is simply not true. Women constantly complain that their men do not help them, talk to them, or share with them (with the exception of bodily fluids), and that in some cases the man's behavior is the epitome of chauvinistic belief. Why is this? It is important for a woman to understand that a man

139

views his mate in a sense of value and worth. Women do this too, but mostly within the simple confine of her man becoming BETTER, as the relationship progresses. Men assign value and worth based on their wants and needs being satisfied. As the woman changes, she tends to leave her man behind, instead of demonstrating the need to change to her man. This causes resentment, and men respond by becoming resistant and confrontational.

In numerous counseling sessions, the following are the most constant complaints of women in this situation:

* He doesn't value my opinion.

* When I suggest we go some place, buy something, or anything in general, he always answers negatively. Then after he thinks about it, he sometimes thinks it is a good idea, but it is always his idea.

* He makes me feel I should feel lucky to be married to him, i.e. financially and materialistically.

* He thinks I should agree with his opinion on everything.

* He lets needed household chores go for weeks before he handles them.

* He has little patience with me; if I ask a simple question, he acts annoyed with me.

* He doesn't care how I feel about things in general. He tells me how I should feel.

* I don't feel loved by him - I don't feel he is proud of me.

* When we are in a crowd, he wants all of the attention.

* He gets mad at me when I don't do things the way he thinks I should.

* He is very negative about my kids. He is also negative about the time I spend with them. To hear him talk about it, he is Mr. Wonderful.

* He acts one way (nice) when he is around people, or family, then another way (complaining or negative attitude) when it is just he and I alone.

* I can never say let's go, or I am ready. He tells me I am controlling.

* When he does something around the house, i.e. cook something; he always has to tell me how he does it; or, when I am gone, he tells me how he cleans the house. He makes me feel that I am not needed, or appreciated, as he can do things much better.

* He has no interest in our house or yard. There are many things I would like to do, but he has a fit every time I suggest anything; saying we don't need it. When someone compliments us on our house, he says he did all of the painting; never acknowledging anything I did.

Doesn't this sound very familiar? In other words, women tend to react to their men instead of, interacting with them. Reaction involves emotional responses, while interaction involves intellectual responses. Because men are resistant to change, women need to do what is required, in order to demonstrate the need to change.

For example, my wife came to me one day and said we "needed" to remodel the kitchen. In my eyes, the kitchen was perfectly fine, but to her it was "icky" (whatever that means) and ugly, and non-functional. My first reaction was; how much it would cost, how long it would take, and why was it necessary - all of which are male reactions. In my mind, the whole idea of remodeling the kitchen was "icky" (I am beginning to like her word icky). More importantly, my wife was attempting to make a point, and it was necessary, on my part, to hear her reasoning. After about an hour of discussion, she outlined how she wanted it designed, all of the new appliances, and the costs associated with the remodel. She had put a good deal of time and effort into this project; she answered all of my questions, demonstrating that remodeling the kitchen was a very good idea, especially since it would raise the value of our home. When she had finished, I told her I thought she had a great idea, and that we should go look at some of the appliances available, and stuff like that.

She had demonstrated to me that this "change" was something that was important. Afterwards, I had no problem with it. I have to tell you, my wife was always very good at demonstrating change to me. It was important to her to interact with me, and she always did a very good job staying away from reacting with me. When she did react to me, she was very quick to realize that only a fight would ensue, and she never wanted to fight. I always noticed she was willing to sacrifice to me, and by doing so, I did everything I could think of to make her happy and sacrifice for her.

She really enjoyed shopping; I hated it, but I would simply look up and say, "Hey, let's go to the mall and check out the puppies, in the pet shop." I could actually see her eyes light up as she ran to get her coat. After a while, I actually liked go to the mall with her because, she simply delighted in looking at everything, and it allowed us to interact with one another. We would look in every store, then go and get a hotdog, sit out in the common area, and talk about everything and anything that came to mind. Then we would go look at everything again. When we got home, she was a happy woman; I could tell when she would hum to herself, that she was content. This is how sacrifice works. I simply could not do enough for her because I knew she gave all of herself to me.

I find, in counseling, one of the most common complaints from women is their mate's unresponsive natures to conversation and spontaneity. Women totally disregard a man's need to recharge his batteries, and seem to always, interpret this unresponsiveness in a negative manner. There are cases where men completely turn-off to their women, but in this instance, it involves more emotional causes, rather than energy deficiency.

Objective thought bothers a woman too. A woman identifies many "grays" in her life, where men tend to see things in either black or white. This manly trait harkens to the protector/security role of men. Battle is methodical and progressive in nature. Organizational skills and task assignment are critical in war. Security concerns are often checked to make sure every facet of the security plan is functioning. Objectivity comes from a man's intellect, and it is there he is most comfortable. Objectivity allows a man to assign tasks as a required chore, priority, and energy expenditure, as a subconscious act. Men even view courtship in this manner. Women view courtships as an experience, men do not.

A man takes in all stimuli into his intellect and expresses it through the physical.

Physical expression is extremely important in a man's psyche. Men express themselves physically in sports, sex, home improvements and repair, auto mechanics, etc. Men also rely very heavily on their intellects and find expression in the arts such as writing, painting, sculpting, teaching, etc. Whatever expression comes out of a man is heavily dependent on a man's maturity, both intellectually and emotionally. The intellect of both genders employs two factors: experiential intellect and empirical intellect. An educated man has a high level of empirical intellect. A man, who is aggressive, or ambitious, usually has a high level of experiential intellect. However, it is easy to see that an immature man will employ these to traits in a wrongful manner.

Maturity in a man defines him as a man. Immature men are really boys in big bodies. Women are drawn to real men like moths to light. Why? Now think very carefully here. What women are attracted to is, the manliness, of a man. Emotionally, they crave intimacy and love, but a big part of that intimacy and love is security and protection. Women need security, and this is why they desire to be a part of the financial planning in a marriage, and part of the decision making process. This defines security and protection, in a woman's mind, not only for herself, but for the children too. Please do not confuse this with a woman desiring to be dependent on a man. This implies that she is simply an object, and I haven't met a woman yet, who desires simply to be an object of a man's affections.

144

Women are also attracted to a man's objectivity insofar, as she generally lacks this trait. Her subjective nature has a difficult time viewing the world from a man's intellectual viewpoint, but many situations call for an objective viewpoint, and the woman is attracted to a man's ability to take charge and provide an answer she would find difficult and cumbersome.

When I first met my wife, she had an eight-year old daughter. About a week after I met her, her daughter did not come home from school. I got a frantic call from my wife so; I went over to her apartment. When I arrived, she had two other girlfriends there, and they were all in a panic. I began to ask questions, to determine her daughter's habits: where she usually went after school, what was her routine, did they have a fight...things like that. I found out that my wife and her daughter had had a fight that morning, so I decided to drive around by her school and trace her path from school to home. It took all of about forty-five minutes, but I found her daughter at a convenience store that was between the school and my wife's apartment. The point I am making here is; that afterwards, my wife appreciated the fact that I took command of the situation, and solved the problem from an objective standpoint. She and her girlfriends were simply too emotional to objectively attack the problem.

Women are also attracted to a man, who is a helpmate. Although social mores attempt to define each gender's role in life, the reality is quite different. Women are very active in the workplace now. Men who willingly help their mates, in all aspects of daily life, find a warm reception from their women, because it demonstrates love and affection.

Women are attracted to men physically, but not in the same way, a man is attracted to a woman physically. Women experience their men physically within their emotions, and this has nothing to do with sex. This, emotional experience of a man, is a unique trait of women, and men cannot begin to understand this trait, since they have nothing to compare it to within their own psyche. Men do not experience the physical aspects of a woman within their emotions. Physical attraction in men is an intellectual experience, coupled with a physical response. What sifts down to a man's emotions are never her physical traits, but it is the essence of the woman, that satisfies a man's wants and needs of a woman. In other words, to a man the physical attraction of a woman is enough to begin a relationship, but for it to continue and eventually, lead to marriage and commitment, the woman must meet or exceed the needs of the man, as he defines these needs. As you can imagine, this may cause some severe problems in a relationship. A man may view himself as loving his woman, while she views the relationship as the man not loving her at all. In counseling, I use a saying that is very important. "Doing your best is sometimes not enough. Sometimes you must do what is required." A man needs to love a woman the way she desires to be loved. This is difficult for a man to understand insofar, as defining how his woman wants to be loved. Once it becomes clear, a man generally has no problem loving a woman the way she wants to be loved.

I hope, as I expand on this subject, you are beginning to see that men and women are two parts to one whole. In other words, what attracts each gender to one another is what is lacking in that specific gender. Men and women complete one another, and marriage is defined as communion, or being one, with each other. Nevertheless, the reality is always different from the perception! The sexes constantly misunderstand the opposite gender because they use words and arguments that have different meanings, within the psyche, that employs these words and arguments. We all speak the same language but we all mean different things. Let me give you an example:

A husband and wife are out, with three other couples, at dinner. All of the attention is focused on one wife, who is the life of the party. Her husband, unexpectedly, says, "Let's celebrate my vasectomy!" His wife looks at him and wonders why he made such a dumb remark, especially when he had had his vasectomy 10 years ago. She is struggling to understand, not only what he said, but also why he said it. She is upset and embarrassed, and when they leave to go home, she lights into him for his stupid remark. She is right to be upset, but she overlooked the fact that her husband was jealous of her being the life of the party, and so he put a damper on it, right away, with his remark. This man is immature, and women have a very difficult time dealing with immature men. His words were misunderstood to mean something that had nothing to do with the conversation. The problem was his emotional immaturity, and if the wife would have known this, she could have dealt with it in a better way, other than lighting into him and causing a fight. As I said before, it is stupid for a woman to engage a man in combat, whether physically or emotionally. She should have waited until they got home, and then sat down with her husband, told him how inane the remark was, and ask him why he had said it. She should have further informed him that it was hurtful and embarrassing too. The husband needs to not only apologize to his wife, but also to the other couples present.

The physical and the intellectual are the only two factors that determine how a man perceives the world around him.
This does not mean a man is not, or cannot be, emotional. This has a very big dependency on the maturity level of a man, which has a good deal to do with his level of intelligence. Mature men use intelligence to solve problems dealing with stress and frustration. Violence comes from immaturity, and anger is nothing more than an ego in jeopardy.

Violent men are immature men! Violence comes from the inability to rationalize a problem and combine it with a rational solution. This takes intelligence and, more specifically, mature intelligence. Violence is a very big response to how the man's mind has been program, which means how the man has been raised. Problem solving is a learned trait. Unfortunately, it is difficult to find adequate teaching in this regard. Maturity is a very big factor, and problem, in today's society. Upbringing is so very important. Most of the cognitive therapy, which is employed by secular psychologists, actually revolves around the re-parenting of the individual. It is necessary to actually start at the beginning, with an individual, and impart certain skills and lessons that were never offered in childhood.

The intellectual and physical response, of a man, defines him as a man. Women cannot view the world in this manner. Since they are multi-task oriented, it is difficult to experience multi-task situations from an intellectual standpoint. Experiencing situations is best accomplished in the emotions. Conversely, female-trained males, find emotional objectivity very difficult. They attempt to employ female traits, with a male psyche, and this produces stress and anxiety.

I grew up in an Italian matriarch family. I was the only boy; and we only had one bathroom. You may want to go get a tissue; this isn't going to be pretty. When I started dating, women were attracted to me, not only because I was a male, but also because I demonstrated many guy-gal traits. In other words, my relationships always seem to dissolve into a guy/girlfriend/girlfriend-type of relationship. I was easy to talk to and be with, but girls never took me seriously as a boyfriend. This was quite puzzling to me, until I entered college, and began studying psychology. I soon discovered, what the problem was, and corrected it, but to this day, I retain the ability to relate to women on an experiencing level; and it has been quite helpful in my career as a behavioral specialist.

I want to point out something here, so there is no misunderstanding. A man employs his intellect and physical expression, from a subconscious level. This does not mean, however, that a man is not emotional, nor spiritual. What it means is a man does not inherently employ these two traits, as a woman would, in the same situation. In my last book, I taught that a man views emotions as relief valves, where a woman views emotions as warning signals. This is extremely important. We will talk about this in detail, in just a moment.

On the spiritual side, a man views his relationship to God in an objective manner. Men do not experience God like women do, but look more to God as an empirical exercise, with corresponding requirements on his part. God gave man a set of laws known as the Ten Commandments. Since laws are most often man-made, man can easily understand that God requires man to obey His laws, and a man can readily transfer authority and control to God because, this is how a man employs his psyche.

Women view spiritual things from an experiential viewpoint. To a woman, God is not an objective exercise, but a subjective experience. In other words, God is more a feeling to women, and they view religion as motion instead of empirical beliefs. Interesting enough, the Christian understanding and belief, in the triune Godhead-Father, Son, and Holy Spirit- the Holy Bible, actually defines the Holy Spirit as the motion of the Godhead. Women can easily identify with this, since experiencing life is a very big part of a woman's psyche.

Men regard emotions as a relief to stress; women view them as warning signs.
We have talked a little about this before, but let's see if I can expand your understanding of this very important difference. If women regard emotions as warning signs, then it follows that when their men are upset and respond emotionally, such as crying, women get upset too, becoming apprehensive and stressed. Immature men often respond to a woman emotionally, causing the woman to respond in turn. Sound familiar? Men may use their emotions in a manipulative fashion.

One of the things I feel I did not make very clear, in my last book, was this emotional aspect of the male psyche. I never meant to imply that men are not emotional, or to imply that women are always emotional. This is not a cut and dried issue; it is more, "how to get the pig through the python" issue. Let me explain...

Remember what I have taught you about the different aspects, affecting the base differences, in both gender's psyches. I cited culture as one, and male-oriented females as well as female-oriented males as another. These causal factors, affecting placebo (or differences which affect the base or placebo model), have a significant impact on male emotions, and how and when, men choose to employ them. Maturity plays a very important role in how a man employs his emotions. Both intellectual and emotional maturity, determine conduct such as, violence, anger, manipulation, etc. What affects maturity? I am of the knowledge and belief that, moral conduct is the underlying cause.

Morals, in both men and women, are a learned trait. A young person quickly learns to either gravitate toward their desires, emotions, and will, developing a warped sense of moral conduct, or he/she learns to gravitate first to the intellect, and hence, develop a very secure sense of moral conduct. This is part of the parenting process, and mentoring relationships.

Presently, I am counseling a grandmother/mother/daughter trio, who are in different stages of co-dependency/addiction recovery/and addiction. All three of them believe the myth that their problems stem from some type of genetic cause. Science has never proved this belief. What science does tell us is that although, genes denote tendency they do not denote action. My premise, that we are always accountable for our actions and conduct, stems from this fact.

Homosexuality has been touted as having a genetic foundation. Once again, we have never been able to prove this in a clinical environment. Homosexuality is a chosen lifestyle, and no one has a genetic proclivity to this lifestyle. I counsel a good many homosexuals, both male and female. I am often asked if my aforementioned premise is true then why do they feel more comfortable as the opposite sex. One man in particular, whom I will call John, told me in one session, "I have no desire to be with women, not socially or sexually. I did not choose to be this way. I cannot believe what you say." I do not question the man's sincerity, in his statement, but making a choice is not always a conscious act. If a person was trying to stab you with a knife, you will make a conscious choice, in your conscious mind, to do everything you can to avoid being stabbed. This is a conscious decision to a threat of danger. But, as I have taught, the subconscious mind makes a decision based on a belief system, which in turn evokes thought. This, process of thought is affected by, intellect, the desires, emotions, and will. Delight is mixed in, affection is assigned to the mix, and what eventually comes out is a set behavior or conduct. Homosexuals, both male and female, employ a belief system, no different from a drug addict. They believe they are different, and they believe they are better off as the opposite sex, and so this is the behavior that is manifested. As I said previously, no clinical information has been able to refute this scenario.

This is no different from the belief that alcoholism is a disease, which is passed down to succeeding generations. There is simply no clinical proof of this. I counsel a good many alcoholics whose children are alcoholics too. I have even some patients whose alcoholism has seemingly

152

passed to the third generation. However, in counseling we discovered this so-called "sins of the father are passed to the son" simply is a myth. The cause of the alcoholism being passed on revolves around the mentoring of the children into a belief system of alcoholism. In other words, being exposed to alcoholism, consistently in childhood, enabled the children to develop a belief system in this lifestyle, at the same time damaging the psyche into believing the father was the cause of the children's problem. It really is a codependency issue and nothing more.

A man is more in touch with his surroundings and has better spatial perception than a woman has.
I use to laugh until I cried, whenever I would ask my wife about anything that had to do with directions. As hard as she tried, she could get lost in the supermarket's aisle. My wife also, never seemed to be aware of what was going on around her. She was a beautiful woman, many guys, would turn their heads to look at her, and every time I pointed this out, she was totally oblivious to the looks and stares.

Men constantly are aware of their surroundings, and are constantly scanning them with quasi-radar, evaluating everything based on security, energy expenditure, etc. This is a built-in, involuntary part of a man's psyche. Women, are easy prey for muggers because, they do not constantly evaluate their surrounding environment. In psychology, we call this "situational awareness." This only applies in spatial relationships, not personal interaction. In personal interaction, women have the men beat. They're more attuned to the emotional nuances of relationships, and this is derived from the nurturing aspect of their psyche.

Let's review what I said, in my previous book, regarding various brain function differences between genders; then I will expand upon it as we go along:

Neuroscience research has established that the two hemispheres in the brain make different contributions to what we know and how we act; although, complex activity requires the entire brain. Left-half cognition involves formal logic; it uses language to interpret what it observes in consistent ways. The left hemisphere's analytic processing -- item-by-item, step-by-step -- conveys the appearance of an objective reality.

The male brain is larger than the female brain, but this does not imply a greater degree of intelligence. Research has discovered that the hypothalamus (the primitive part of the brain), in males, is five times larger than in females. Although the female brain is smaller, women use more of their brain; in fact, both hemispheres, and we know this fact by what is called the "corpus callosum," or the mass of white transverse fibers connecting the cerebral hemispheres of the brain. In women, the corpus callosum is 40% larger than it is in men. When the two hemispheres of the brain have the ability to communicate with one another, through the corpus callosum, consciousness occurs. Research also tells us that, men have a stronger left-hemisphere brain function than women, and this is where logic, reasoning, and rational thinking take place. This is why men take everything in through their intellect, and this is also why, they are progressive in thought and objective in nature.

In contrast, right-half cognition works according to a situational logic. Its information combines bodily perception and active imagination. It creates patterns, or mosaics of meaning, by a leap of imagination. The left-brain specializes in an explanatory way of knowing, the right, in an experiential way. Each is necessary; neither is sufficient by itself.

The right-hemisphere is where women excel, over the men, in such things as verbal fluency and comprehension. Women tend to talk better, and express better, than men, and learn foreign languages more easily than men learn. They are better at expressing their feelings, and tend to gravitate toward experiencing life, rather than compartmentalizing life as men do. The greater size of the female corpus callosum indicates that, women have a more highly developed ability to better integrate reason and intuition, and to search for harmony and peace. Intuition is foreign to men, and men actually discount this quality of women to a point of disbelief.

While these generalizations apply to male and female brains alike, brains may also vary according to gender. "Essentialist" gender theory, maintains that men and women are essentially different *(duh!)*, and that these differences are related to the brain, much more than to culture. Because girls' capacity for language (located primarily in the left-brain) matures earlier than boys', they rely more on verbal skills in solving problems, including nonverbal problems, such as spatial tasks. In boys, however, the right hemisphere, which specializes in spatial-perceptual processes, matures earlier than it does in girls. Boys rely more on physical movement and spatial perception, in engaging the world, than on language skills.

As it applies to speaking, and making hand movements that contribute to motor skills, women tend to be more focally organized than men. Girls generally speak earlier, articulate better, and have better fine-motor control. More women are right-handed than men, but when it comes to abstract tasks, such as defining words, men are more focally organized than women.

The earlier development of the left hemisphere, in girls, enables both hemispheres to handle information in similar ways. The left-brain processes nonverbal information, as well as verbal; the right brain uses verbal strategies, as well as nonverbal strategies. There is less division of labor, less specialization between the contributions of each half.

People with greater symmetry -- usually but not always female -- are more dependent on the situation in which they find themselves, and more sensitive to the context, especially its interpersonal nuances. These individuals respond to subtle experiential clues, which interfere with the process of abstraction. Perhaps that explains, in part, why a right-brain quality, like intuition, is more prevalent in women than men. Their interpretive capacity more easily, senses and voices, what is happening with both hemispheres. Information is more integrated than discrete. At the same time, an equal distribution of functions creates a liability: the person is less able to hone in on a few details, which are relevant to a pattern.

Research has also linked certain disabilities with hemispheric differences. Autistic, reading-disabled, and mathematically gifted children are most often male, left-handed, and prone to immune disorders including allergies.

Those children (usually male), who start talking at a later age, show an extreme separation between their verbal skills and their nonverbal abilities. Instead of each hemisphere being a generalist, as is true of early maturers, each hemisphere specializes either in an analytic, or integrative, strategy. The right half handles perceptual information, the left conceptual information. In a male-dominated society, the male role is reinforced by the time of puberty.

Perceived reality is highly affected by environment and family upbringing. Actual reality is inherent in the situations, or physical surroundings, you find yourself in. Perceptual information may be misunderstood, conceptual reality acts as a given.

The late-maturing male, growing into the male-dominant social world, can succeed, or conquer, with his narrowed left-brain view of the world. He is in the right place at the right time. Regardless of the fact that he may be working with a specialized half brain, the world is his; he made it.

But what if the male, in the example above, grows up in a female-dominant family? How does this fact alter his identity? I alluded to this earlier, using my own childhood as an example. I can remember all too well reacting to everything my sisters did. I was outnumbered and the battles were sometimes very fierce. If my sisters weren't stealing my clothes, talking on the telephone, living in the bathroom, or blasting their record players, they were huddled together thinking of ways to make my life miserable. Nevertheless, reacting to each and every situation was plain wrong. Reaction is emotion and emotion does not work in situations of conflict. Interaction involves intellect; only when you identify a problem, and rationally think the problem through, will a solution present itself.

The problem, then, is the woman's...or is it? How can she be female (using her more generalized processing pattern), and still function in a social world, shaped by a male-related way of specialized processing? Some females learn to adapt their processing skills accordingly. (On the other hand, men today may feel a demand to change their particular style of processing to include women's distinctive participatory style.)

Men and women also, of course, share perceptions of the world -- here is a street; this is a Bible; those are the stars. Both sexes adjust to cognitive differences, and with age, women and men become more androgynous (*having both male and female characteristics*). However, because the brains of women and men may differ, in the basic features I have described, they often construct different worlds, and have different understandings of the realities they find themselves in, at a given time.

Here is the most astounding difference between the male/female psyches. Because each gender perceives the world differently, and because each gender constructs a different world from the stimuli coming into their minds, each gender views the world differently than the other. Social mores tend to define each gender's position in a relationship. Women, for example, are to tend the house, cook, take care of the children, etc. Men, on the other hand, are to be the breadwinner, handle repairs, do chores, and be the spiritual head of the family, etc. However, these so-called positions have pretty much become a fallacy, but both genders tend to hang on to them, even when they do not work and are not true. More and more women have entered the workplace today. But, with that said, more often than not, it is because the family unit has been saddled with debt to a point where the wife's income is desperately needed. Also, women have a need for success and accomplishment, especially male-oriented females. This has caused the home scene to require a sharing of duties, within the home. Women need the help; men want to relax. A woman will react to this example purely with emotions. In her mind she does just as much to provide income as the husband, hence, he should work just as hard within the home as she does. The husband doesn't see it this way, especially if the financial burdens of the household were caused by the wife's inability to check her shopping expenditures. This is pure reaction, people!

Who is correct in their thinking? This isn't a test; there is no correct or incorrect behavior. I see only selfishness and immaturity. If you love your spouse, and something is bothering your spouse; WHY would you resist changing what is bothering your spouse. If your wife cannot stand the smell of booze and cigarettes, why as a husband in love with his wife would you subject her to both things? Even if some of her demands are frivolous or inane to you as a man, LOVE IS SACRIFICE AND THAT MEANS SACRIFICING THE GOOD AND THE DUMB THINGS TOO.

And ladies, many times, I see the problem of how a wife talks to her husband as perpetuating the problem. Men may not see the problem as you do, and they may not even see the problem at all, but you can bet on the fact that a man sees very quickly, just how his wife talks to him. It is either respectfully, or it is not. Men are not children, but women tend to treat them as such. I have found men to be resistant to change, just to dig their heels in and resist, because of the way the wife reacts to him. Interaction involves respectful speech and patience.

For example, many men have minimized the importance of "women's intuition." They claim that an experiential approach to knowledge easily falls into subjective bias. In contrast, feminist thinkers tend to view, with suspicion, anything, which claims objectivity. They value personal experience as an important source of knowledge, and believe that men distort what they know, when they don't acknowledge their personal experience, and histories.

It is easy to see that the battle of the sexes is founded on the different ways we think and perceive. But if not understood, anxiety, confusion, and frustration may occur. The very act of fantasy occurs in how we seek relief from this anxiety, confusion, and frustration. This is not only endemic in male/female relationships either. Anything that causes a person anxiety, confusion, and frustration may trigger fantasy. It all depends on how we have been trained to deal with these factors. In other words, the emotional and intellectual maturity of an individual is the most determining factor.

The body produces certain chemicals in the brain known as endorphins. Endorphins cause the body to react to stress, fear, and sex. Both men and women possess endorphins that the other gender lacks. Women tend to have more serotonin, and men have more dopamine. Depression is more prevalent in women, and research has found that depression is related to serotonin levels in the brain. Schizophrenia is more prevalent in men, and research has found that schizophrenia is related to dopamine levels in the brain.

This clash reflects different perceptions of what "experience" is. Perceptual origins also affect knowledge. In the physical and human sciences, knowledge has come from "distinctive and often perverse masculine understandings of only masculine social experience."

In a man-made world, women are forced to live their lives as square peg beings, jammed into a round hole existence. Have a heart, fellas! It isn't easy being a woman. Your masculine view of the social experience is not hers. Women look to their men to provide many things lacking in their psyches. They want spiritual leaders, security, someone who will experience life with them, protection, and love. Men often perceive they are providing all of the above, but it is not what you perceive, it is what she perceives. Remember the famous battle cry of my last book. "Doing the best you can is sometimes not enough; sometimes you must do what is required."

Each and every woman, on the planet, has defined, for herself, how she wants to be loved, and she is constantly looking to see if her man loves her in this way. And it is not as simple as just sex; intimacy is important, but intimacy for a woman is the effect of being loved "her" way, not the cause. Plopping your butt in a chair and watching football is not part of the solution; it is part of the problem. Selfishly pursuing habits that are offensive and hurtful is immature. Where is the love? What is it you sacrifice for your lady? How do you make her feel loved? What emotional security do you provide her? Please note I said "emotional security." A nice house, and car, is not emotional security. You cannot "stuff" her psyche away, and expect your wife to be happy and content, within the marriage, when you selfishly ignore her emotional and physical needs.

"But what about me?" you cry. Okay, what about you? When you said, "I do." that meant, "you would" provide for your wife's needs. Some of those provisions require sacrifice. Some of these provisions may be alien and strange, but doesn't make them go away. You must do what is required and, in turn, your wife will do what is required to make you happy and content.

Now it is the woman's turn. Be nice! Do not treat a man like a child. Physical and emotional conflict with a man is just plain dumb! Nagging and coercion will not get you what you want and need. Patience and dialogue will. Demonstrating the need for change is needed for a man to change. Understand your man; allow him to rest; then ask for his help. Intimacy is important to a man, and when a man feels he has lost value and worth, in his wife's eyes, he is very resistant in all aspects of the relationship. I can remember when I would complain about the endless list of chores my wife had for me to do, and I would balk; she would always say, "Take your whiny, pouty butt, and take it outside." She was very adept at avoiding confrontation with me. Even when I came looking for a fight, she would smile and give me a hug and say, "Why do you behave as if stupidity is a virtue?" I would laugh until I busted a gut. I simply could not get my wife to engage me in battle. And she was very clever in getting me to do the things I should have been doing in the first place. She knew I love cookies, so she would bribe me in order to get me to do a major chore. If I were out doing chores around the house, she would come out and help me, which usually turned into a water fight, or some other prank. We had great fun together; her most sterling quality was that she never took life seriously. There was always a time for fun. Is there a time for fun with your husband?

The processes, which involve a blurring of the boundary between subject and object, have come to be associated with the feminine, and the posture of "objectification" associated with the masculine. Thus, "truth itself has become genderized." As a system of beliefs, science has also acquired a gender, affirming the masculine value of objectivity, rather than a more broadly human value like participation.

Remember what I have taught about belief systems. They evoke thought and, in turn, evoke behavior. If belief systems have become "genderized" then it, follows that truth, or the belief systems, employed between genders are quite different and, in turn, evoke different behaviors. I can believe in God no differently than a woman can believe in God, but my perception of God, as a man, is different than a woman's perception of God, and so this is an example of genderized truth.

Women's experiences seem to be ones of "continuity," with their social and biological realities. In their quest for truth, they became what they already symbolized: "the fleshly, the nurturing, the suffering, and the human." Instead of inverting what they were (most likely they didn't have that choice), they deepened what they were. Their symbols disclose less contradiction, and more "synthesis and paradox."

It is easy to see how conflict enters a woman's life, and if not handled properly, will become addictive behavior. Being "one" with something is communion. Women commune with their social and biological realities in a way that is alien to men. In other words, women are very comfortable and content with being women, as long as they are around other women. They are not comfortable being women around men and, this is because both men and women no longer commune with one another; they, more times than not, simply companion with one another.

Women gave the concept of "human" a meaning beyond the dichotomy of male and female. Because of their sense of continuity, with life, a concept of "other" played little part. They drew on symbolic aspects of life, closer to their ordinary experience -- eating, lactating, and suffering.

Women appropriated the dominant view of the cosmos in a way different from men, and with different implications for both. Because men were high and lifted up, they needed to be brought low, "to renounce their dominance." Women, however, deepened their ordinary experience "when nature impinged upon it. (Pain in childbirth)" Their bodies not only served as "a symbol of the humanness of both genders, but also a symbol of -- and a means of approach to -- the humanity of God."

Women have a need to bring men down to their level of thinking; not necessarily usurping the man, but bringing him into an area where they can better understand the man. Somehow, this all got messed up and from an acceptance perspective, women feel rejected from the male-dominant view of reality. This needs to be corrected and realigned properly. Men constantly misinterpret this need, to bring them into their understanding, as an attempt to change and manipulate them. This is wrong! Men need to understand that the world is man-made, and women are struggling to understand the world from their subjective respective. Men are objective in their approach to life, and women find objectivity difficult. Do not make the mistake of viewing your woman's attempt, to understand better, a male-dominant world, as an attempt to manipulate.

A similar contrast in religiosity is evident today. Women's experience of God tends to deepen their own humanity, making the everyday sacred, while many men experience a longing to overcome their humanity.

Women strive to become intertwined spiritually; men attempt to view spirituality objectively, as something that is a higher authority. Women internalize spirituality; men externalize it. Women view God subjectively and make God a part of their emotions. Men view God objectively and make God a part of their intellect.

Brain research shows the brains of men and women are organized differently, and these gender-related but not always gender-specific, differences could be construed as suggesting new stereotypes, another "dichotomy." That is not my intent. Neither sex, alone, bears "the image and likeness of God," only the species does.

This cannot be mutually exclusive, in terms of identity. As we continue, we will see that we will always be two parts to one whole. God, in the book of Acts, of the New Testament, says that He is not a respecter of persons. In other words, there is neither male, nor female, in God's eyes. In fact, God makes it quite clear that in heaven, there is no such thing as marriage, since there is neither male, nor female, in heaven. The Bible is filled with both men and women characters, and both are depicted in good and bad settings. We rise or fall on our own laurels. We, as different genders, have different roles in life. How we live within these roles is most important. Social mores constantly skew the way we view these gender-related roles. However skewed these roles become, in a man or woman's mind, theses specific roles have not changed over time; it is we who have changed.

In studying the subtleties of male and female differences, future brain researchers may eventually assist us in creating a model of behavior that we can call fully "human," and truly "godlike" -- the male personality balancing the female in his being, and the female balancing the male in her being -- one image, of equal but different parts, representing one humanity.

Two parts to one whole, people. This is one of the roles, which I spoke about, that will never change! The historical concept of, male/female gender, dates back to the dawn of man. Just what are a male and a female anyway? People readily identify the sexual implications to my question, but struggle with the deeper definitions. This question speaks more of fact than fallacy. Identities are skewed today, and both genders have a difficult time struggling with identity issues. What is needed is a frank conversation between the man and the woman over this issue. Many couples have poor communication skills. It is so very important to talk things through, to hash out the issues that constantly confront a relationship.

A man tends to be more focused on single types of actions and goals, and is easily annoyed when interrupted.
Women have the uncanny ability to think and do many things at once. This part of the female psyche actually drives men nuts. They have nothing in their own respective psyche to compare this trait to, and consequently; they have very little ability to relate to women on this level. With that said, women need to understand the objective nature of men, and their need to

assign tasks and progressively accomplish these tasks. When a man is interrupted, he must begin again, in progressive steps, to pick up where he left off, prior to the interruption. Women find this male trait exasperating. They constantly view their men through their own emotional filter. Women want to be loved their way, interact with their men their way, do all the things they normally do, their way, and when their men cannot respond their way, they have a tendency to feel and act in a manner that results in stress and anxiety. In psychology, we call these stresses and anxieties, gender-triggered problems. Both sexes need to sit back and make a list of the things their mates do that they do not like. Then examine each one to see if they are gender-triggered problems. Here is a list of common gender-triggered problems, I have compiled, from my case studies, and my responses to these problems.

1. She only wants to talk to me when I am doing something I like to do.

2. He does things like smoking, when he knows I don't like the smell of smoke.

3. She is constantly badgering me to spend more time with the kids.

4. He never wants to do anything except watch television and have sex.

5. She won't let me relax; she always has a list of things for me to do.

6. He won't talk to me; if I say something he doesn't like, he gets up and leaves.

7. She always wants help. I never ask her to help me.

8. He has the manners of a slug, and says things in front of other people, that are hurtful.

9. She is constantly telling her girlfriends about our marriage, and personal things.

10. He is such a hypocrite; in public, he is Mr. Wonderful, but at home, he is an ass.

11. Everything I do and say, in public, is wrong. She is constantly criticizing me and harping on me.

12. He talks to me like he is my boss. Everything is an order.

13. She talks to me as if I were a child. I already have a mother; I don't need another one.

14. I don't feel he loves me; I don't feel we are close to one another.

15. She is constantly seeking reassurance. I am doing the best I can; I don't know what else to do.

Yep, all of the above basically sums up the most often said, complaints I hear from my patients. Now I want to take them one at a time, and attempt to explain each one as it pertains to both gender's viewpoint. Take what you have learned so far, about the male psyche, and try to follow my reasoning. Later, when we discuss the female psyche, all of this will fall into place.

1. She only wants to talk to me when I am doing something I like to do.

If you remember, I have taught that men are progressive in thought, and object oriented. The male psyche cannot think along multiple planes as a woman can. A man must constantly concentrate on single-task goals, and may become quite annoyed if interrupted. The way a man responds to interruption is predicated on his maturity. Women are constantly interrupting their men, and this really is a matter relegated to courtesy. As I said before, my wife used to, constantly, interrupt me, when I was writing. She was not being rude; she was being a woman who wanted to communicate with her husband, but just seem to pick the wrong times to communicate. I wouldn't get angry; I only had to look up from my keyboard, with a questioning look, and she would apologize and walk away. It is important to note that when this occurred, and after I had finished writing, I would go and seek her out and ask her what she wanted to talk about. This is important because women need to know that their voice is appreciated and, since women are highly communicative, they experience life by communication. Many times, what my wife wanted to talk about, were seemingly unimportant things, which could easily evoke anger. What is important to a woman is not necessarily important to a man. In one particular instant, my wife wanted to ask me if I thought she should cut her hair differently. Most men do not care about their wives hair; only that they have hair, so this is an example of an interruption that could easily evoke an angry response from a man. However, as I said, maturity plays a big part in this scenario. It would serve no purpose to castigate my wife over this question. Why? Even though her hairstyle meant little to me, on the surface, it meant a great deal to her; so because I loved her, it did mean a great deal to me. Vanity issues and beauty are very important to women. They have a strong desire to be perceived as beautiful, to their men, and to others because, a woman's psyche operates within the emotional plane. When women get together, they experience one another by sharing beauty secrets and clothes, etc. Men do not do this because they are more intellectual in their pursuits, and express things physically. Please, DO NOT take this to mean that women are superficial. This is simply not true. Sharing experiences is a big part of the female psyche. This sharing is a sense of security. When men get together, they may talk about tools, and sports, or home improvements, but they do not share themselves with one another like women do; they simply exchange information.

2. He does things like smoking, when he knows I don't like the smell of smoke.

In a particular counseling session, with a husband and wife, the wife made this a very vocal complaint. She went so far as to refuse to have sex with her husband if he smelled of smoke and drink. I simply asked the husband if he loved his wife, and he answered "yes." My response, "Then why do you do things to upset her, if you love her?" His response, "Because she talks to me as if I were a child." Now listen closely. In psychology, we call this situation a "parenting problem." Just because you are grown up, and live in an adult body, does not mean you are an adult. She did one thing he didn't like, and he responded doing something that she didn't like. Sound familiar? If you come to a locked door and you do not have a key, do you stand there waiting for the door to open, or do you look for another entry. In other words, if you dislike some behavior in your spouse, and your

170

complaints fall on deaf ears, do you continue to harangue your spouse? I pulled the wife aside and put this exact question to her. She saw the logic in what I said, but didn't know how it could solve her problem. This is what I told her, "Your husband knows your complaint, and he is quite comfortable in his rebuttal, so change up on him." She looked at me questioningly so I continued, "You won't have sex with him when he smells of smoke and drink, and we both know he is quite verbal about your refusal. He wants sex so, instead of yelling at him like you would a child, tease him." The wife smiled and said, "You mean tease him sexually?" "Yep, and get him so hot he can't stand it. BUT, do not give him sex unless he stops smoking and drinking. Good behavior only gets the reward." Well, the wife did just what I said and called me, about three days later, to confess that she was having the time of her life, teasing her husband. It got to a point where he knew what she was doing, and actually enjoyed it too. In all of my years of practice, I have never seen a man stop smoking and drinking, as quickly as I did that husband. (As an aside, the wife was an islander from Guam, and she was a "knockout" looking woman. I would have cut off body parts, if she were my wife. Hahahaha!) The moral to this story is to changeup they way you respond to your mate. Everyone puts up defenses, for all types of situations. In order to get by the defenses, you must change your tactics. Remember, the poets say the heart is a lonely hunter? And remember my response to this wrongful belief? Hunting is for fools who have never heard about bait. The wife, in the above example, changed her tactics and began to bait her husband, by teasing him. If he wanted sex, he could have all the sex he wanted, but he had to stop smoking and drinking. Bait 'em ladies, it works!

3. She is constantly badgering me to spend more time with the kids.

Listen up guys, a woman, who spends all day with children, needs a break, and needs to be with adults. I have two daughters, and there were times when I came home, where she [my wife] would run out of the house and jump in her car, just to get away from them. She moved so fast, she leaned into her turns like a motorcyclist. Have a heart, fellas! There is no excuse for not helping with the children, and the mentoring relationship is so very important here. Not only does a woman need a break from the kids, she is very concerned, if the husband refuses to spend time with the kids. Kids need their dads to balance their perspective of the world. This is an essential part of child rearing. Male and/or female-orientation of opposite genders is causing some severe identity issues today. Sons, being raised by their mothers, need a male mentoring perspective. Daughters, being raised by their fathers, need a female perspective. Please do not deny your kids this needed growth perspective. I have already explained that I grew up a female-oriented male. No girl took me serious, as a boyfriend, but I was a great guy-gal companion. My father was never around, and to this day, I have very little interest in sports or other male pursuits. My father simply did not provide this type of male perspective. I grew up with my mother and sisters. I can still gab with the best of them, but I actually had to parent myself, when it came to the male perspective.

4. He never wants to do anything except, watch television, and have sex.

What's wrong with watching TV and rutting? Just kidding...sheesh! Many times men gravitate to TV to get away from their spouses. Men easily live within their fantasies, and this can be dangerous if left unchecked. Remember, a man needs to rest and recharge his batteries, but not for more than a few hours. Anything, over and above, this has some other underlying issues that need addressing. Remember the lesson about the husband and wife (above), and his smoking and drinking; women who constantly nag their husbands will either, evoke a combative response, or a withdrawal response, from their mate. Retreating to the TV can be a withdrawal response. Quit nagging and bait the man, dear.

5. She won't let me relax; she always has a list of things for me to do.

Men have a tendency to gravitate toward a mindset that, since they work all week long, the weekends belong to them. Wrong! The weekends belong to the family, and chores are a big part of the family interaction. Men also have a tendency to be lazy. But do not confuse this trait, with one where the man just cannot perform maintenance type tasks. I am one of those men who cannot fix anything. I am all thumbs, when it comes to car mechanics, or household tasks; anything I take apart and fix, actually works when I am finished, but I always seem to have a ton of leftover parts. Amazing! I may be able to fix things, but it takes me so long to figure mechanical things out, it actually isn't worth my time; so, I always tend to hire a handyman to do these things, and practice trickle-down economics. Plus, my work schedule is very long and tiring, and the last thing I want to do, after a fourteen-hour workday, is come home and fix something. My wife always seemed to understand that I wasn't good at fixing things, especially when I turned her washer into a bucket of worthless junk: so she just went, and called someone instead of, me destroying her stuff. It cut me, but I got over it in about two seconds! Hahahaha! However, guys who can fix things should do so, and should get the kids to help. It is excellent training for them, and it provides a good mentoring situation. It also provides the biggest mess on the planet but, hey, I am not God; I am only a psychologist!

6. He won't talk to me; if I say something he doesn't like, he gets up and leaves.

It is all in the way you present things, women. Combat is a very big part of the male psyche, and men are good at it. If a man "perceives" his mate to be degrading him, or talking down to him, he is going to respond in a combative manner. Bait 'em ladies! Change up and present your needs differently. Do not constantly nag a man. Keep him off balance and take away his defenses. Women are actually very good at this. My wife was a, superstar pro, at getting me to do things. She would fake lifting heavy items, knowing I would go to help her, and then she would tell me there was more heavy stuff, in the garage. Four hours later, the garage was cleaned and she was nowhere to be seen. Amazing! Another time, she told me we were going to go a party, but we needed to make one stop. I am all dressed up and an hour later, we had a new sofa. She was very, very good! When I would fake complaining, about her "bait and switch" tactics, she would smile that one smile, only reserved for husbands, and say, "Take your whiny, pouty butt and take it outside."

7. She always wants help. I never ask her to help me.

This is a very big complaint from men, and it is simply because they do not understand the female psyche. Women want to experience life, especially with their husbands. Interaction is very important to a woman, and she will do just about anything, to get it, including asking for help when she really doesn't need it. Men will find if they have good interaction with their wives that this "asking" for help goes to a minimum.

8. He has the manners of a slug, and says things in front of other people that are hurtful.

Boy, where have I heard this complaint before? Men will say things to evoke a reaction from their wives. But never, is this an excuse to be hurtful...NEVER! Love does not hurt; it builds the other person up. I am a comic; my wife used to complain that I said things, to evoke laughter, that were hurtful to her. I was devastated! The one particular instance that comes to mind was at a dinner with three other couples, and I remarked, "I don't know what my wife does all day. She has a gardener to take care of the outside of the house, a maid who tends the inside, and cooks and a nanny who take care of the children. All she needs to do is hire someone to have sex with me, and she is out of a job!" It caused a good deal of laughter, but it offended my wife tremendously, and boy did I hear about it when we got home. I called each couple on the phone and apologized for my stupid remark, and hoped I didn't offend anyone else at the dinner. I then sent flowers and a teddy bear to my wife; she forgave me, but I was always very careful when I

175

attempted to be funny at her expense. Also, there are no excuses for bad manners. That is your woman, fellas, and she is the queen bee, so treat her like a priceless gem. Women really enjoy good manners and being made to feel special; who wouldn't? I like my back scratched, so my wife always would come up, unasked, and scratch my back. She liked foot massages, and I would reciprocate, unasked, and she just delighted in the attention. When it gets right down to the practical details, I would do just about anything to make my wife happy and content. I noticed when she was happy, I was happy; when she was upset, I was stressed.

9. She is constantly telling her girlfriends about our marriage and personal things.

Ladies, this is a part of your experiencing natures, but this is also one thing that is highly offensive to a man. Men do not like personal information exposed, especially when it comes to intimate details of the marriage. It is a security issue with men, and stems from the hunter/protector role of their psyche. Marriage is a private affair, and should remain private between both spouses. This is not to say that men do not violate the privacy issue either. Men are just as much at fault, and women react in a negative manner.

10. He is such a hypocrite; in public, he is Mr. Wonderful but at home, he is an ass.

I hear this lamentation an awful lot. Women desire to admire and respect their men. They tend to become quite vocal, when their men display hypocritical traits because; it lowers the value and worth of a man in a woman's eyes. Women need to realize that a good many men fantasize about their lives, but more often than not, the fantasies engaged are ones where the man feels he has not been successful and/or lived up to his potential in life. Sexual addiction is a very big problem with men, which generally has its roots in adolescence. A young man, who trains his mind in sensual things, finds it very difficult to overcome the need for sensual fantasies. These fantasies portray their owners as something they are not, and they spend a good deal of time walking up and down in these fantasies. They have a desire to act out these fantasies to people they come in contact with, and although they always fear becoming exposed, they always move on to a new group of people to fool. Wives find this trait almost intolerable, and rightly so. You can never live a life in reality, when you are constantly living a life of fantasy. Women marry based on their men's ability to get better. Women have a terrible time handling a situation where their men become worse. Co-dependency is a big problem among women today. They have a tendency to blame themselves for their husband's actions, and this is very, very wrong. Women who find their husbands becoming a hypocrite need to get professional counseling, which is to include the husband, if possible.

11. Everything I do and say, in public, is wrong. She is constantly criticizing me and harping on me.

I do not know a man who is not prideful; and even though pride is classified as one of the deadly sins, it is a man's inherent nature to be prideful. Men do not tolerate disrespect from anybody, let alone their wives. Men believe strongly that a wife should support them and be their biggest fan. This is not a healthy belief. A wife is not a "yes" person, and in my own marriage, my wife did not hesitate to put me in check where she thought I was wrong, HOWEVER, she accomplished this in private, not in public. I remember one time my wife and I were going to a charitable function, with four other couples. We had all chipped in and bought a table. Being a comic, it is easy for me to get everybody laughing, and loosen up the group, so to speak. This one particular time, my wife dared me to quit acting like an "idiot" in public, and made me promise to keep quiet so I did. About 30-minutes into the function, the other couples began to wonder what was wrong and then asked if I was ill. I told them what my wife had said; their reply was like this, "What? I only came to this function tonight because I knew you were coming, Jay. You can't be serious?" So, my wife relented and released me from my promise, and I proceeded to act like an "idiot" the rest of the evening. Men need to realize that women criticize them based on how they "perceive" others viewing them. Men discount women's intuition; having nothing in their own psyche to compare this to, so they pass it off as irrelevant. Women are very perceptive, and are usually "right-on," in their perceptions. However, being right-on doesn't give a woman license to demean her husband in public. Do not do this ladies; men are great at combat and will engage you in public.

12. He talks to me like he is my boss. Everything is an order.

I have seen this trait, in men, so many times; it is actually no longer amazing to me. Wives can be submissive, but they are equal, in the partnership called marriage. Each gender has a role to play in marriage, and no one role supersedes the other. Women are to be cherished, not demeaned by a dominant male figure. This goes both ways too. Maturity plays a very big part in this equation. Many women accept male-domination in order to receive

178

love. This is co-dependency, ladies and it is wrong. Whenever I slipped up and started sputtering orders at my wife, she would always say, "Jay, I think you got me confused with the dog. Remember, I am the one you have sex with." Actually, after a couple of scotch and sodas, the dog doesn't look half-bad. I'm kidding! There was just no way my wife was going to let me get away with playing brigadier general in our family, and no woman should allow it in theirs either. Gentlemen, God made women from your rib, not from the soles of your feet. They were not created as slaves, but equal helpmates. Please do not tread on them and view them as the weaker sex. I am here to tell you, my wife had a left hook that came outta nowhere!

13. She talks to me as if I were a child. I already have a mother; I don't need another one.

We have already addressed this in a previous example, but suffice it to say that women need to examine how they talk to their husbands and make sure they are courteous and respectful. Men need to do this too, and this is one example where both parties need to practice what is so much needed.

14. I don't feel he loves me; I don't feel we are close to one another.

We have also addressed this problem, but please remember we all want to be loved the way we want to be loved. Both spouses may think their mates know they love them, but this simply is not true. Do not practice the golden rule with your mate; practice the platinum rule" "Do unto your spouse as they want it done unto them!"

15. She is constantly seeking reassurance. I am doing the best I can; I don't know what else to do.

Women are constantly seeking security and reassurance. Like I said previously, sometimes doing your best is not enough. Sometimes you need to do what is required. Your spouse defines what is required. This definition is the way your spouse wants to be loved. My wife really enjoyed touching. She craved touching and caressing. Sometimes, I thought, she couldn't get enough of it, but it was so very easy to love her this way because I enjoyed it too. Men, who understand the female psyche, find it easy to love their wives in the way they want to be loved. Women completely take their men into their emotions, and cannot separate these emotions with rational and intellectual behavior, as men do. Love is an emotional experience for a woman, while men view it as a physical experience. To understand the mystery of a woman is to understand her emotional needs. This side of a woman completes a man, by providing a man the part he is lacking in his own psyche. My wife did this very thing for me. Intimacy with her cannot be put into words, and I was never capable of intimacy like she displayed. There is nothing in God's green world that even comes close to the intimacy of a woman. Get out of your head, gentlemen and into your heart and learn the most cherished lesson a woman can offer her man. Learn to love!

A man is externally oriented, as it pertains to his surroundings.
He is constantly evaluating his surroundings, in order to gauge safety, success, problems, opportunity, and most of all energy expenditure. His decision processes are all governed by this systematic "radar-like" scanning and assessment. Because he is task and object oriented,

interruptions and "things" not in their proper place, easily frustrate him. Men are constantly being accused of being "anal" when they are simply programmed this way. Men are very good at noticing things that happen, physically, around them, but fail horribly with subtleties and innuendo. Body language, implied meanings, intuition, or anything subjective in nature, are difficult for men to understand. Everything has its place in a man's world, and he is easily frustrated when things aren't in their proper place. This does not just apply to physical things, but also intangible things too. My wife was famous for, using one of my tools, and then it disappeared forever. It was nowhere to be found. When I asked her where it was, she would just shrug her shoulders and say, "I can't remember where I put it down." I am the only guy on the planet who has purchased 5,056 hammers in my lifetime. I used to hang it on the pegboard in the garage. Now I hide it so no one can find it. It was actually easier to go and rent a storage unit, to put my tools in, just to protect my investment. Another thing my wife couldn't do involved directions, and knowing at all times, where north, south, east, and west were. Do you know those freeway signs that say, "Bakersfield North," for example? They would confuse my wife to a point of tears. She always seemed to end up in San Diego, which was okay, but we lived in Los Angeles.

To a man, love is more a physical expression than an emotion.

Women constantly complain that men confuse sex with romance, and they do...they really do. Romance, being more of an emotional exchange, is a woman's domain, and men have to try hard to satisfy this womanly delight. Women delight in romance because they spend a good deal of time in their emotions. Hey, I think I am on to something here. However, with all of that said, romance is not love; romance is one of the effects of love. Love, to a man, has more than a physical expression; it has a place. Sound familiar? Courting is a very much a task to a man, but not in a negative connotation. Courting requires time, energy, and the expenditure of resources. A man would never explain it this way, to a woman, unless he wants to die alone, but this is exactly how a man subconsciously evaluates courting. The equation for love, for a man, is to physically become attractive to a female, ask her out, discover if she meets his needs, spend a good deal of time with her, and then ask her to marry him. Between spending time and popping the question, the essence of the woman is sifted down to the man's emotions and becomes embedded in them, and he is in love. A man, who violates this courtship equation, is a man who is in LUST. When a man is physically attracted to a woman and they sleep together, this actually prolongs the man's lust, and when he tires of it, the relationship usually ends; more often than not, it does not result in marriage. When a man is physically attracted to a woman and she DOES NOT sleep with him, it is this very mystery that causes her essence to sift down to the man's emotions and, eventually, he pops the question. Men fall into LUST first, and then LOVE! Rarely does lust become love; because the sifting down of the woman's essence does not occur, and there is a very big difference between physical attraction and love, to a man. A man who sleeps around is a lustful man, with very shallow values, and little desire for permanency in his life. He is also a selfish man, since there are diseases out there that can kill his sexual partner, as well as himself, but both seem not to care. I use a saying, quite often, when I teach young people in my "Teen Idols" seminar. Would you lend your bathing suit to some other person? Of course not, because of the hygiene issue, so why would you lend your body to another person? Social mores have changed the way men and women interact, but the mind still works the same way. Casual sex relationships damage the psyche, and callous the mind, to a point of distrust for the opposite gender. This is a very severe problem, and I counsel people every day, over the damage done by physical relationships. The female psyche suffers the most in this type of relationship. Because the female psyche spends most of its time in the emotions, women tend to take a failed relationship harder than men. The word "morals" today seems to imply something nasty or unneeded. You only have to listen to the victims of these broken physical relationships to understand how necessary morals are. I teach both genders that they need to develop a "rulebook" and stick to it. This rulebook guides their life in all situations.

Women complain that men spend too much time in their mind and not enough time in their heart.
The term "heart" here, implies emotions. This is very true, and when a man does "spend" time in his emotions, he tends to intellectualize them and express them physically. This bothers a woman; I have taught that, women view emotions as warning signals. In fact, I will go so far as to say this is one of the leading problems that women have with men. Women experience life through an emotional plane. Men do not do this, but intellectualize life through a physical plane. Think! One gender completes the other, since it provides what the other gender lacks. But, if what I say is true, why do we

183

not come together so easily and why do we seem to do the opposite of what we were intended to do? These are important questions, and I want to be very articulate here.

When I say men take everything in through their intellects and express them physically, what I mean is that, they "filter" all incoming stimuli through their intellects, and express them physically. Men do have emotions and do have a spiritual side to their psyches, but everything is first filtered through their intellects, and then assigned to the other three aspects of their psyches. Let me use myself as an example. I am constantly being accused, by the lady in my life, my daughters, and my sisters, of always staying within my mind. As a psychologist, I see some pretty outrageous inhumanity being practiced, some of which evoke a tremendous emotional response from me; but it is first filtered through my intellect. I cannot separate my emotions from these situations; they are there and they are real, but these same situations are intellectualized first, and then acted on emotionally. When I get together with my guy-friends, for a football game party, my lady looks at me as if I fell out of a truck; she is actually stunned at some of my behavior. She never sees me get physical with anything, but there I am giving my buddies "noogies," and shoving them around, yelling at the television, etc. She is so used to seeing me in a professional demeanor that when she sees me acting like a little boy, she is shocked. Many times, when we drive home, she is very vocal about it too. "I cannot believe you took off your shirt and tried to strangle Jimmy, just because he won that bet from you. Have you lost your mind? What has gotten into you?" So, filtering stimuli through a gender-based plane is a good deal different than acting within a given plane (Jimmy lived, by the way).

To a man, his wants are determined by what he can have.

This is so very important. In men, it is simply a matter of desire versus resources, which includes energy consumption needed to obtain it. Men view acquisition very, very differently than women. Men see something they want, and if resources allow them to get it, they do. Women see things they want but it doesn't necessarily trigger acquisition. This is why women can go window-shopping and men cannot. If I go to the mall, with one of my daughters, I am going to buy something. My daughters can go to the mall, and spend the day, coming home empty handed. Amazing! So, whenever my daughters need to buy something, they take me along, knowing I will buy it for them. Hey, there seems to be a pattern here...

Men do this with women too. A man is attracted to a woman physically first, wanting her sexually and romantically. But resources will always define if he "makes his move." The term, resources, refer to more than money in this particular case. I have taught that men view courting as a task. Women take offense to this because they do not understand the male psyche, but you really cannot blame them. Who wants to be viewed as a task? When I met my girlfriend, I had to move a good deal of work aside to be with her. I am constantly adjusting my schedule to be with her. Sometimes I am so exhausted from, my job; I simply cannot find the energy to do some of the things she has planned. She is very understanding; however, many times I can hear the disappointment in her voice, or see it in her eyes, so even when I am exhausted, I try to find the time and energy, rather than disappoint her.

I want to point out another important distinction. The terms "wants" and "needs" are very different in meaning. A man actually determines his wants by what he can have. In other words and this is important, a man formulates his wants in his mind, based only on what he can have, as he sees it. I may want to be the king of France in my fantasy, but in actuality, this is not a want because I know this is impossible. I don't even speak French! I can kiss in French, but that is about the extent of it. Women do not view wants in this manner. Women view wants subjectively, where a man views them objectively. Women can experience things, and desire them, but this is not necessarily considered a "want," nor do they determine these wants based on what they can have. They determine wants based on what they can experience. In other words, experiencing it is enough for a woman; where it is not for a man. A man wants it! A woman wants to experience it! When a woman experiences something, and it isn't enough, it then triggers acquisition. I have watched women shopping in a jewelry store. They can try on jewelry, simply delighting in how it looks on them, and then move on. If you watch them closely, it is only when they return to some piece that they had tried on earlier, do you see acquisition triggered in them. Jewelers know this and train their salespeople to, always watch for when a woman returns to an item.

This acquisition trait, in women, also protects a woman from falling in love quickly, and pregnancy, for that matter. It is nature's way of protecting women, much to a shallow man's remorse. Men can fall in lust in a

186

nanosecond. I timed myself once; it took all of about a blink of an eye, for me to fall in lust with my girlfriend. Wow! Hubba bubba, baby! But love took a few more blinks. If more women had the morals of my girlfriend, the world would be a much better place. I lost my wife six years ago, and it was very difficult for me to find love again. When I did find it, my girlfriend made sure it was she, who defined terms and boundaries. In other words, to my girlfriend, no ring on the finger = no sex; and no situations that could potentially lead to sex either. I can actually tell you the first time we held hands, and let me tell you, my head almost exploded. My girlfriend is an expert at keeping the mystery alive in our relationship. You should see her rulebook: no smoking, no drinking, no swearing (try doing this at a football party), no groping, and no heavy breathing. I was lucky to get the woman to kiss me and, oh, no French kissing either, until she was ready. Many guys would say, "Forget it" and move on. They receive exactly what they seek; I got what I wanted. What was initially lacking, physically, in our relationship, she made up for in loving and caring. No one, on the planet, does loving and caring, better than my girl! Keep the mystery alive ladies. Intimacy should evolve with the relationship; not define it. Keep a strict rulebook; it will pay off. I have never been intimate with my girlfriend, but just try to keep me away from her. She does it right!

To a man, someone, or something, has to be in control.

Men exercise control by using intellect and physical power; to a man, something, or someone, always has to be in control. If not, or in other words, if the man "perceives" that someone, or something, is not in control, then the man will assume control of the situation. Women absolutely abhor this trait in men. To a woman, control is expressed by design and purpose. If you were to sit in on a female executive meeting, you would be hard pressed to determine just who was in control. This would not be the case in a male executive meeting. The male boss usually, sits at the head of the conference table; where the female boss sits next to the person she communicates well with, and has the best relationship with. In a female meeting, they talk about anything and everything, but in a male meeting, everything is progressive and assigned to an agenda. The most interesting aspect between the two meetings is that in the female meeting, they tend to get more accomplished.

Whenever male and female executives work together, it is necessary to define who is in charge. Men will assume they are, if not determined in advance, and this causes the female to resent the male. Taking it one-step further, if the female is in charge, but does not demonstrate to the man that she is the boss, the male will usually attempt to take charge. Because the female executive controls by purpose and design, it is her nature to get the people around her to participate in accomplishing the task(s) set before them. Men misinterpret this need for group participation to mean the female does not want to be in control, so the male attempts to grab control. This is a very wrongful misinterpretation.

Control is considerably more important to a man, than it is a woman. It is not in a woman's nature to be dominant. It is very much a part of the male psyche to be dominant. The biggest lamentation, I constantly hear, from women is, "He always has to be the boss. Why can't he treat me as other women do, and just be equal with me?" The reasons, ladies, are that a man defines the word "equal," differently than the way a woman does. Equal, to a man, is treating women like one of the guys, and this is not what women want. A man treats other guys with a view of domination in mind. Women want to be treated the "same" as other women treat them, and this is not natural for a man. This is a learned trait, and it is learned based on a man believing he needs to learn this trait. Remember, men change based on their belief that they need to change. Women very rarely attempt to dominate other women. They are comfortable "competing" with other women, but very rarely want to dominate. Men relish competition and domination, and this is why men fight wars.

Authority is a given in a man's mind.
A private, in the US Army, knows without being told, that a colonel outranks him, and so every time a colonel walks by, he salutes him. In a father/son relationship, the son knows how to act because the lines of authority are given, in his mind. When a father/son relationship goes bad, it is usually caused by a lack of respect for authority, or a resistance to authority. Resistance is also very much a part of the male psyche. To a man, someone, or something, has to be in control, and if the man determines in his mind, that the person, or thing in control, is not worthy of control, the man will resist. However, this resistance is also evaluated based on resources and energy consumption. In other words, even resistance is filtered through the normal processes of the male psyche.

If resistance is impossible, the male psyche will then seek to identify something meaningful with the situation. During World War II, the Nazis conducted vast amounts of experimentation, on Jews in the concentration camps.

They found that when a man views resistance as futile, but is assigned tasks that are meaningful, they set about to accomplish the task: even if it is something that helps the enemy. However, if they are assigned tasks that are inane, and without meaning, the Nazis found that this would actually drive the prisoners insane.

Josef Stalin, the Russian dictator and murderer, understood human nature very well. It is said that in one of his meetings, with his generals, he took a live chicken and plucked all of its feathers out in front of them. He then went and fed the bird some food. Even after suffering such physical trauma, the bird still took the food and did not attempt to flee. In hopeless situations, the mind attempts to find something meaningful to its existence.

Men normally intellectualize their emotions, and always express them in the physical.
Fantasy, hence, can bring violent reactions in men. Men will fantasize solutions to their problems, while women emotionalize their problems, without an attempt to solve them. Fantasy plays a big part in the male psyche, but this is not the case in the female psyche. Women tend to fantasize about things that are obtainable, in real life; men fantasize about things they perceive as unobtainable. I had a male patient who believed he was a coward. His fantasy, was viewing himself as a five-star general, in the army, with about thirty Medal of Honor awards. Conversely, I had a female co-dependency patient, whose husband was a sexual addict. She blamed herself for his problem, and her fantasy was being more sexually alluring and loving, to her husband. Blame has a good deal to do with how each gender employs their emotions, and we will discuss this in a moment.

It is easy to see that, men make up the largest number of addicts, of all types. However, they are also the easiest to break of addictions. Female addicts emotionalize their addictions, and take a considerable amount of time to learn how to intellectualize them, to a point where a counselor can break them away from them. Female addicts are the worse addicts. Men spend a considerable amount of time within their fantasies, and this is very dangerous. If left unchecked, they attempt to act out their lives within the fantasy. My patient, who I referred to earlier, who thought he was a five-star general, actually went out and bought a uniform and the medals, and would spend the day going out in public; performing (as he thought a five-star general should, in public). Unfortunately, for him, there are laws against impersonating a general officer of the US Military, and he got into big trouble because of his acting out his fantasy.

It is quite easy for men to act out their fantasy, and quite pleasurable to them to do this. Women simply cannot understand this trait in a man, and become easy victims, to men who are quite good at doing this. A boy, who begins looking at pornography, becomes addicted to sensual things; this leads to masturbation, then prostitution, and eventually, a fantasy life of self-gratification, selfish pursuits, insecurity with women, and a variety of other problems, of a sexual nature. Any time, whatever sexual act is employed by the fantasy, is not providing a big enough thrill, the addict graduates to the next step, which is always something more perverted and/or depraved. I once counseled a very distraught wife, whose husband constantly viewed her in various disgusting sexual acts, and attempted to act these fantasies out in their love life. He would place her in handcuffs, and do some disgusting things to her. In a fit of tears, one session, she asked me how a healthy man views sex with his wife, and this was a very good question. An addict, always views real life filtered through his fantasy. A healthy man, views sex with his wife, as an expression of love, with only his wife. His mind is not fantasizing about another woman, as he is making love to his wife. We have a term for this kind of behavior. We call this vaginal masturbation. Most wives would be very surprised at how often this actually occurs. A good many, so-called, healthy marriages experience this unfortunate problem, but it goes unchecked in most cases. Do not get me wrong; women do this too, and fantasize about having sex with another man, while engaging in sex with their husbands, but nowhere near the degree to which men do this.

Men always require a fantasy to masturbate, but this is not the case for a woman. To a man, masturbation is viewed as a failing, and shame always occurs, after the act is accomplished, except for the most calloused of mind. To a woman, masturbation is simply a release, and shame may occur, but more often than not, it does not. Men and women view masturbation, in each other, very differently. Women take a poor view of men who masturbate, and usually blame themselves for the men's behavior. Men view women who masturbate as a "turn on," and are more ready to accept this act in their women.

When men blame, they look for external causes.
Women look for internal causes. I have a very famous saying regarding blame, "Blame is a useless concept!" Why? Because it provides an excuse for our conduct and behavior, and life only offers choices, not excuses. I am

192

going to attempt to tie in various ideals I have taught so far, and this is so very important.

The concept of blame was the inherent flaw in Freud's protocol of "psychoanalysis." Freud believed that all adult behavior stemmed from childhood causes. Most of his protocol was correct, but not all behavior stems from childhood, and this actual belief system has enabled many people to blame their adult problems on circumstances, which occurred in their childhood, or for things their parents did to them, or for their upbringing in general.

The inherent flaw in blaming others for problems occurring in your life, centers on the idea of control. We have discussed how each gender views and employs control in their lives. Blame transfers control of your life to another person or entity. For example, when my daughters would fight, I would usually have to break it up, and when I asked them what was going on, I would get a response like, "Jamie took my toy so I hit her." In other words, my daughter, Jennifer, used Jamie, taking her toy, as an excuse to hit her sister. How many times have you reacted to someone who has made you angry? How many times have you reacted to someone who has done you wrong? My daughter, Jennifer, was wrong in saying that Jamie made her hit her because she took her toy. The correct statement would have been, "Jamie took my toy and I chose to hit her." In other words, reacting to a situation is your choice. Reaction is usually wrong because it, more often than not, involves an emotional reaction, which is usually immediate in nature. Interacting, using your intellect rather than your emotions, usually results in making a correct choice. BUT, IN BOTH SITUATIONS, CHOICE IS ALWAYS

EMPLOYED! And this very act of choosing causes another person to exercise control over you. My wife hated it when her mother would lay a guilt trip on her, and cause her to do something she did not want to do. But, when she spoke to me about this, she did not like me to point out that all her mother was doing was controlling her. She was very adept at taking her frustration out on me too. And this is exactly what her mother was doing. You choose to react or interact. No one makes you angry; you choose to get angry. In the Bible, there is a passage attributed to Jesus Christ, which says, "It is not what goes into a man that makes him unclean, but what comes out of a man that makes him unclean." It was not the guilt that my mother-in-law spoke into my wife that caused her to do the things she did not want to do, but it was the choice my wife made, to accept the guilt, and believe in it, and then choose to respond in a controlled manner to it. YOU CONTROL YOU! YOU ARE ALWAYS ACCOUNTABLE FOR YOUR CONDUCT AND BEHAVIOR! Blame is useless!

Both men and women practice manipulation, very extensively in their lives. It is a very big part of both gender's psyches. However, the way manipulation is acted upon, is very different in each gender. Women always internalize blame, and men always externalize blame. Women tend to blame themselves for many things that occur in their lives; men always tend to blame others. Because of this important, gender-related trait, women make-up some of the worst co-dependents. Men, on the other hand, are rarely co-dependent.

Men think progressively and desire their wants and needs to be met progressively.

194

When this doesn't occur, it triggers anxiety and confusion. Men may often retreat into their fantasies when this occurs; the norm is to work it out. Let me give you an example: A male sales executive loses a big account, and is called on the carpet for the loss of this profitable piece of business. Instead of reviewing and correcting what caused the customer to go somewhere else, he drowns his troubles in drink, and strengthens an already bad drinking habit, which if left unchecked, will lead to alcoholism. The cause of his behavior was NOT losing the account; that was the trigger. The cause was in the way he handled the failure. He intellectualized the loss, as a personal failure on his part, instead of realizing it was due to his lack of attention and expertise, which is important in any career. In other words, he is emotionally immature. He took what was intellectualized, and turned it into an emotional judgment.

Here lies the inherent flaw in both gender's psyches. We know certain things are harmful to us, but we never seem to be able to control ourselves. Through our intellects, we find excuses and rationalize our judgments, even of things, which are harmful to us. Here, once again, maturity plays a big part, but it goes much deeper than this. We are intelligent beings, created to employ both our intellects and emotions. Why do some people make poor choices, while others make good choices? And with all things being the same, why do some family members become "black sheep," and others go on to great achievement? Why do we always seem to gravitate towards feeling bad, or being made to feel sad?

In my last book, I cited the 5th century theologian St Augustine's lamentation over this very point. This flaw is not a new trait, within both gender's psyches. It has been a part of us since the fall of Adam and Eve, in the Garden of Eden. As I have pointed out numerous times, and have repetitively hammered home, is the fact that we become whatever we believe. The foundation to all behavior and conduct is our belief systems. This is a very big truth, but even secular psychology has recognized the exception to this rule. They call it cognitive dissonance. This is where our actions are inconsistent with our beliefs. I went to great lengths to describe this contradiction in my last book, but I want to expand on this subject because it is one that most often confuses my readers.

I can offer no better example of cognitive dissonance than the great lamentation of the Apostle Paul, in the New Testament Book of Romans Chapter 7. Biblical history has recorded for us how even the greatest Christian, of all times, was miserable over the effects of how cognitive dissonance had kept him in a life of bondage, and away from achieving what he held dear. Listen...

Rom 7:1 Know ye not, brethren, (for I speak to them that know the law,) how that the law hath dominion over a man as long as he liveth?

Rom 7:2 For the woman, which hath an husband, is bound by the law to her husband so long as he liveth; but if the husband be dead, she is loosed from the law of her husband.

Rom 7:3 So then if, while her husband liveth, she be married to another man, she shall be called an adulteress: but if her husband be dead, she is free from that law; so that she is no adulteress, though she be married to another man.

Rom 7:4 Wherefore, my brethren, ye also are become dead to the law by the body of Christ; that ye should be married to another, even to him who is raised from the dead, that we should bring forth fruit unto God.

Rom 7:5 For when we were in the flesh, the motions of sins, which were by the law, did work in our members to bring forth fruit unto death.

Rom 7:6 But now we are delivered from the law, that being dead wherein we were held; that we should serve in newness of spirit, and not in the oldness of the letter.

Rom 7:7 What shall we say then? Is the law sin? God forbid. Nay, I had not known sin, but by the law: for I had not known lust, except the law had said, Thou shalt not covet.

Rom 7:8 But sin, taking occasion by the commandment, wrought in me all manner of concupiscence. For without the law sin was dead.

Rom 7:9 For I was alive without the law once: but when the commandment came, sin revived, and I died.

Rom 7:10 And the commandment, which was ordained to life, I found to be unto death.

Rom 7:11 For sin, taking occasion by the commandment, deceived me, and by it slew me.

Rom 7:12 Wherefore the law is holy, and the commandment holy, and just, and good.

Rom 7:13 Was then that which is good made death unto me? God forbid. But sin, that it might appear sin, working death in me by that which is good; that sin by the commandment might become exceeding sinful.

Rom 7:14 For we know that the law is spiritual: but I am carnal, sold under sin.

Rom 7:15 For that which I do I allow not: for what I would, that do I not; but what I hate, that do

Rom 7:16 If then I do that which I would not, I consent unto the law that it is good.

Rom 7:17 Now then it is no more I that do it, but sin that dwelleth in me.

Rom 7:18 For I know that in me (that is, in my flesh,) dwelleth no good thing: for to will is present with me; but how to perform that which is good I find not.

Rom 7:19 For the good that I would I do not: but the evil, which I would not, that I do.

Rom 7:20 Now if I do that I would not, it is no more I that do it, but sin that dwelleth in me.

Rom 7:21 I find then a law, that, when I would do good, evil is present with me.

Rom 7:22 For I delight in the law of God after the inward man:

Rom 7:23 But I see another law in my members, warring against the law of my mind, and bringing me into captivity to the law of sin, which is in my members.

Rom 7:24 O wretched man that I am! who shall deliver me from the body of this death?

Rom 7:25 I thank God through Jesus Christ our Lord. So then, with the mind I myself serve the law of God; but with the flesh the law of sin.

Even Paul knew that "something" was warring against his mind. He also knew that the battle for life is in the mind. No greater problem affects mankind than cognitive dissonance. As I pointed out in my last book, cognitive dissonance is not anything mysterious; it is simply the mechanism the mind uses to change a prevailing belief system; however, with that said, it more often than not, changes the belief system to one that is wrongful. So how do we guarantee ourselves that we can employ the proper belief systems? This is the one million dollar question so sit back and listen very closely because, great minds have studied this problem for centuries, and now it is time to give you back that, which is yours...your life.

Men set boundaries, and most laws are man-made, not woman-made.

Men are more comfortable within boundaries because of their instincts to protect and preserve. Everything has a place, to a man, but this part of the male psyche actually drives women nuts. Society, as a whole, is a man-made organization, designed to protect each member from harm, and to attempt to organize people along the lines of security, safety, allocation of resources, and the pursuit of happiness. Laws have been employed to punish those who do not choose to follow the goals of each particular society. Societies have evolved, over time, from family, clan, and tribe, to nations of the world. Every society has an inherent culture, which is richly steeped in traditions and ideals that have evolved over the centuries. These cultural influences are very important to the belief systems we employ.

The ancient Israelites took the Ten Commandments, of the Old Testament, and expanded them to 613 laws, which governed the lives of all Jews, from ancient biblical times, up until and including today. Every society has had its system of laws. The Roman Empire was known for its laws and its "Pax Romana," or peace it evoked, and many societies since, have patterned its system of laws after that of Rome. Laws have been the tools all societal structures have used to bring peace, social order, and security to the society that employs them. But let's not forget that all systems of law are man-made and not woman-made structures. Women, since the dawn of society, have been forced to live out their lives, within various systems of law, defined by their respective cultures, and designed by the opposite gender.

This organization of society, defined and implemented by man, has had a terrible influence and impact on the development and employment of the female psyche; only within our lifetimes, has this begun to change. As women worldwide, demand more and more freedom that belongs to them, to develop and influence their respective societies, many times this is viewed by the men as an assault on their male freedoms and domain. Feminism has reared its ugly head, and there is a very substantial difference between, feminism and womanhood. We were never meant to attack one another. We were made to attract one another, and complete that which is lacking in the opposite gender.

The battle of the sexes will continue as long as one gender views, or perceives, the opposite gender as an enemy, out to destroy or usurp, the inherent rights and roles, each gender positionally possesses, and this is a terrible wrong. As more and more women enter the workplace, men continue to perceive this as a threat, and this is simply not true. Equality in the workplace is a very big problem today. Women do not wish to be treated like one of the guys, but they do wish to be treated as an equal member, when it comes to compensation, benefits, and credit for a job well done. I have personally, worked with a good many female executives, and I have found them just as competent as their male counterparts. Culture has a good deal to do with this misperception too. Men have had the title of "breadwinner" for centuries, but the "Leave It To Beaver" days are over. Economic considerations are forcing many women into the workplace. Male-oriented females, raised by their fathers, view themselves as completely capable of doing male-type jobs. Cultural considerations will always have a tremendous influence on the way both genders react or interact.

In boys, the right hemisphere, which specializes in spatial-perceptual processes, matures earlier than it does in girls.
Neuroscience research has established that the two hemispheres in the brain make different contributions to what we know and how we act, although complex activity requires the entire brain. Left-half cognition involves formal logic; it uses language to interpret what it observes in consistent ways. The left hemisphere's analytic processing -- item-by-item, step-by-step -- conveys the appearance of an objective reality.

In contrast, right-half cognition works according to a situational logic. Its information combines bodily perception and active imagination. It creates patterns, or mosaics, of meaning by a leap of imagination. The left-brain specializes in an explanatory way of knowing, the right in an experiential way. Each is necessary; neither is sufficient by itself.

While these generalizations apply to male and female brains alike, brains may also vary according to gender. "Essentialist" gender theory, maintains that men and women are essentially different *(duh!)*, and that these differences are related to the brain much more than to culture. Because girls' capacity for language (located primarily in the left-brain), matures earlier than boys', they rely more on verbal skills, in solving problems, including nonverbal problems such as, spatial tasks. In boys, however, the right hemisphere, which specializes in spatial-perceptual processes, matures earlier than it does in girls. Boys rely more on physical movement and spatial perception, in engaging the world, than on language skills.

The earlier development of the left hemisphere, in girls, enables both hemispheres to handle information in similar ways. The left-brain processes nonverbal information as well as verbal; the right brain uses verbal strategies as well as nonverbal strategies. There is less division of labor, less specialization between the contributions of each half.

People with greater symmetry -- usually, but not always female -- are more dependent on the situation in which they find themselves, and more sensitive to the context, especially its interpersonal nuances. These individuals respond to subtle experiential clues, which interfere with the process of abstraction. Perhaps that explains, in part, why a right-brain quality, like intuition, is more prevalent in women than men. Their interpretive capacity more easily senses and voices what is happening with both hemispheres. Information is more integrated than discrete. At the same time, a more equal distribution of

202

functions creates a liability: the person is less able to hone in on a few details, which are relevant to a pattern.

Those children (usually male), who start talking at a later age, show an extreme separation between their verbal skills and their nonverbal abilities. Instead of each hemisphere being a generalist, as is true of early maturers, each hemisphere specializes either in an analytic or integrative strategy. The right half handles perceptual information, the left conceptual information. In a male-dominated society, the male role is reinforced by the time of puberty.

Note: Perceived reality is highly affected by environment and family upbringing. Actual reality is inherent in the situations, or physical surroundings, you find yourself in. Perceptual information may be misunderstood, conceptual reality acts as a given.

The late-maturing male, growing into the male-dominant social world, can succeed or conquer with his narrowed left-brain view of the world. He is in the right place at the right time. Regardless of the fact that he may be working with a specialized half brain, the world is his and he made it.

Note: But what if the male, in the example above, grows up in a female-dominant family? How does this fact alter his identity?

The problem, then, is the woman's...or is it? How can she be female (using her more generalized processing pattern), and still function in a social world shaped by a male-related way of specialized processing? Some females learn to adapt their processing skills accordingly. (On the other hand, men today may feel a demand to change their particular style of processing to include women's distinctive participatory style.) Men and women also, of course, share perceptions of the world -- here is a street; this is a Bible; those are the stars. Both sexes adjust to cognitive differences, and with age, women and men become more androgynous (*having both male and female characteristics*). But because the brains of women and men may differ in the basic features, I have described, they often construct different worlds and have different understandings of the realities they find themselves in at a given time.

For example, many men have minimized the importance of "women's intuition." They claim that an experiential approach to knowledge easily falls into subjective bias. In contrast, feminist thinkers tend to view, with suspicion anything, which claims objectivity. They value personal experience as an important source of knowledge, and believe men distort what they know, when they don't acknowledge their personal experience, and histories.

Note: It is easy to see the battle of the sexes is founded on the different ways we think and perceive. However, if not understood, anxiety, confusion, and frustration may occur. The very act of fantasy occurs in how we seek relief from this anxiety, confusion, and frustration. This is not only endemic in male/female relationships either. Anything that causes a person anxiety, confusion, and frustration, may trigger fantasy. It all depends on how we have been trained to deal with these factors. In other words, the emotional and intellectual maturity of an individual is the most determining factor.

This clash reflects different perceptions of what "experience" is. Perceptual origins also affect knowledge.

In the physical and human sciences, knowledge has come from "distinctive, and often perverse, masculine understandings of only masculine social experience." The processes, which involve a blurring of the boundary between subject and object, have come to be associated with the feminine, and the posture of "objectification" associated with the masculine. Thus, "truth itself has become genderized." As a system of beliefs, science has also acquired a gender, affirming the masculine value of objectivity, rather than a more broadly human value like participation. Women's experience seemed to be one of "continuity" with their social and biological realities. In their quest for truth, they became that which they already symbolized, "the fleshly, the nurturing, the suffering, and the human." Instead of inverting what they were (most likely they did not have that choice), they deepened what they were. Their symbols disclose less contradiction and more "synthesis and paradox."

Note: It is easy to see how conflict enters a woman's life, and if not handled properly, will become addictive behavior.

Women gave the concept of "human" a meaning beyond the dichotomy of male and female. Because of their sense of continuity with life, a concept of "other" played little part. They drew on symbolic aspects of life closer to their ordinary experience -- eating, lactating, and suffering. Women appropriated the dominant view of the cosmos, in a way different from men, and with different implications for both. Because men were high and lifted up, they needed to be brought low, "to renounce their dominance." Women, however, deepened their ordinary experience "when nature impinged upon it (pain in childbirth)." Their bodies not only served as "a symbol of

the humanness of both genders, but also a symbol of --
and a means of approach to -- the humanity of God."

*Note: Women have a need to bring men down to their
level of thinking, not necessarily usurping the man, but
bringing him into an area where they can understand.
Somehow, this all got messed up, and from an acceptance
perspective, women feel rejected from the male-dominant
view of reality. This needs to be corrected and realigned
properly.*

A similar contrast, in religiosity, is evident today.
Women's experience of God tends to deepen their own
humanity, making the everyday sacred, while many men
experience a longing to overcome their humanity.

*Note: Women strive to become intertwined spiritually,
men attempt to vie spirituality, as something that will
make them better. Women internalize spirituality; men
externalize it.*

Brain research shows the brains of men and women are
organized differently, and these gender-related, but not
always gender-specific, differences could be construed as
suggesting new stereotypes, another "dichotomy." That is
not my intent. Neither sex alone bears "the image and
likeness of God," only the species does.

*Note: This cannot be mutually exclusive in terms of
identity. As we continue, we will see that we will always
be two parts to one whole.*

In studying the subtleties of male and female differences,
future brain researchers may eventually assist us in
creating a model of behavior we can call fully "human"
and truly "godlike" -- the male personality balancing the
female in his being, and the female balancing the male, in

her being -- one image, of equal but different parts, representing one humanity. The historical concept of male/female gender dates back to the dawn of man. Just what are a male and a female anyway? People readily identify the sexual implications to my question, but struggle with the deeper definitions.

Men marry based on a woman satisfying his wants and needs as he defines them.
He is first attracted physically, to a woman, courts her to establish commonality and satisfaction of his wants/needs, and marries her; once again, using progressive steps. As the marriage progresses, he sees his wife in a constant state of change. He may even view this change as a violation of the marital vows, since he agreed to love the woman he married, not this new person. Change bothers men! A woman needs to understand this male trait, and employ change gradually, while at the same time, demonstrating progressively that change is good. Men basically look for two things from a woman: Respect and admiration + Love. When a man's needs are met and the essence of the woman has sifted down to a man's emotions, the man will ask for marriage.

Regarding women...
Now, let's begin by expanding on the topic of traits identified, regarding women. From the dawn of mankind on this planet, women have been mistreated, abused, taken for granted, humiliated, and quite a few other adjectives, but I think you get my point. It has only been in the last hundred years where the plight of women has been brought into the light, and attempts have been made to correct this terrible injustice. But, allow me to make myself perfectly clear, men are not completely at fault for the plight of womanhood today. As mankind attempts to

correct this problem, women are just as much at fault in their attempts to perpetuate it by the way they dress, the way they act, the way they attack, and the way they skew their understanding of the male psyche. There is a very big difference between womanhood and feminism.

Socrates, the so-called great Greek thinker, viewed women as, lower than slaves, who at the time of Socrates were the lowest caste in Greek society. The Pharisees, of the New Testament Bible, would pray to God, thanking Him for creating them as men and not publicans, gentiles, or women. I find this very amazing indeed, and as I pointed out in my last book, the ancient Hebrews have a saying, "Isha Tisov Ev Gener," or "A Woman Surrounds A Man." The Israelites of the Old Testament got it right; a woman was created to complete a man. The subsequent generations, of the New Testament, had it terribly wrong; women were not created as chattel or property. The Arab cultures today still view women in this manner.

About eleven years ago, Rodney King, the black man who was beaten by Los Angeles police officers, uttered a statement, in an interview, that has been chanted by millions. He said, "Can't we all just get along?" To ask this question is really to answer it. The battle of the sexes will continue, until we learn to understand the opposite gender. Like I said, opposites attract, not attack.

The way a man views a woman can be the very seed sown for battle. In addition, the way a woman reacts to this seed can be the cause that perpetuates the battle. As I said previously, strength is made perfect in weakness. The strength of man resides in his intellect. Power is its counterfeit and resides in the emotions. A woman corrects the weakness of man and in turn, man grows stronger. God tells us that a woman was created for man. A woman completes in a man what he lacks. What he lacks is the understanding of communion. As man continues to live by the soul, he will continue to, lustfully view women wrongfully. God corrected the problem of communion versus companion in His plan of salvation, which was to return man to His divine system of communion. To do this God gave man a woman to demonstrate this communal state and sent His only begotten Son, to the Cross- to redeem mankind. This salvation plan is finished. Now we must use what has been so graciously given, and learn to interact with one another and live as one. So let's begin to learn about, in my opinion, THE most marvelous creature God ever created...WOMAN!

A woman thinks on a multi-linear plane.
Women tend to have multiple thoughts going through their mind at one time, which to a man, would be overwhelming. This one of the leading causes of non-communication between genders. Even I am forced to admit that I have talked to women, who have wearied me to a point of near exhaustion, by talking rapidly and on multiple subjects. Simply put; men cannot keep up, and their only defense mechanism is to not engage women in conversation.

A woman takes in outside stimuli into her intellect first, like a man, but then transfers it immediately to her emotions.
While there are only two factors that make up the framework of the male psychology, a woman has four: intellect, physical, emotion, and spiritual. These four traits act as filters, and what comes out of a woman is not the same as a man.

Women express things using four criteria and men have a difficult time understanding the emotional and spiritual sides of the female psyche.

The emotional aspect aside, the gender differences regarding the spiritual are profound. Men view God as a set of laws; the ever-present need for boundaries in a man's life never goes away. Women view God as an experience and tend to look at God as a relationship. Women's experience of God tends to deepen their own humanity, making the everyday sacred; while many men experience a longing to overcome their humanity.

A woman internalizes, or is internally oriented, in the way she conducts her life.

Women must force themselves to concentrate on single-task functions because this does not come naturally for them as it does in men. Women do not see things in simple black and white like men. They tend to see beyond existing parameters.

Women see beyond the confines of set limits, where men stop at these very same limits.

As I said previously, boundaries are important to men. Hence, men place limits in their lives and tend to operate within the confines of these limits. Subconsciously, men continuously evaluate everything based on energy expenditure.

To a woman, love is more emotional than physical.

A woman falls in love by taking in the outward stimuli of attraction, but not into her intellect. She takes it immediately into her emotions, where it is churned, as the relationship progresses, until it finally embeds itself as a seed and then love begins to grow. In other words, a man must enter into a woman's emotions first, similar to the physical sex act, but performed mentally, in order for a woman to fall in love.

The love of a woman "completes" a man as the man enters her emotions and fills her inner being.
Women fall in love easier than men, and this is why women do not view sex from a physical plane like men. This is a natural protection from pregnancy.

To a woman, the concepts of "wants" and "resources" are two very separate ideals.
Men view their wants as something to "acquire" as soon as resources are available. This is not the case with women. A woman may be attracted to something, or SOMEONE, but not necessarily want it or desire to own it. Women, statistically speaking, make the worst addicts. They tend to emotionalize everything they take into their psyches, and consequently are the hardest addicts to cure. Men, on the other hand, intellectualize what they take into their psyches and express them in the physical. This type of behavior is more easily arrested and eventually cured.

Women control based on purpose and design.
A man lives out his life either by, being in control, or transferring control, to another person or entity. Women don't do this. They base control on simple factors of direction or purpose. When a woman's emotions completely give out, she will transfer control to her fantasy, as relief from anxiety, depression, or other emotional trauma, resulting once again in addiction.

Control is not a given in a woman's mind.
In a mother/daughter relationship, control is not so much a given. It is more of a concept of direction and purpose, and is viewed as an inherent value in the relationship.

This explains why many mother/daughter relationships seem to be ones of conflict and mistrust. The mother's purpose and direction for her daughter's life is seemingly quite different than what the daughter's purpose and direction is, and since women control using purpose and direction, a conflict of desire occurs.

Women emotionalize everything so their reactions to conflict are expressed through their emotions.
Men are objective in nature, and view emotions as unnecessary subjective reactions. But as women experience life; men simply live it. And they live it primarily in the physical too!! Women experience life through their emotional plane and hence they emotionalize everything they do. This is not a negative because women need this attribute to sustain the nurturing side of their psyches. You almost never hear of a female serial killer; child molestation rarely involves female perpetrators.

Where a man turns an intellectual problem into an emotional judgment of personal failure, a woman in the same situation, wrongfully interprets her emotion as a lack of acceptance.
Acceptance is very important to a woman. They spend a lot of time communicating, looking for acceptance, on many different planes at once.

Objective reality comes easy for a man, but is a tremendous limitation to a woman.
Women have a tendency to operate beyond their reality.

Women think subjectively; hence, women see their behavior having many different causes and are able to justify all of them emotionally.

212

Objective thought, which is man's way of thinking, causes a man to rationalize everything he does within his fantasy.

Women tend to view, with suspicion anything, which claims objectivity.
They value personal experience as an important source of knowledge, and they believe that men distort; what they know, when they don't acknowledge their personal experience and histories. This reflects different perceptions of what "experience" is. Perceptual origins also affect knowledge. In the physical and human sciences, knowledge has come from "distinctive and often perverse masculine understandings of only masculine social experience."

The processes, which involve a blurring of the boundary between subject and object, have come to be associated with the feminine, and the posture of "objectification" associated with the masculine.
Thus, "truth itself has become genderized." As a system of beliefs, science has also acquired a gender, affirming the masculine value of objectivity, rather than a more broadly human value like participation.

Women's experience seemed to be one of "continuity" with their social and biological realities.
In their quest for truth, they became that which they already symbolized, "the fleshly, the nurturing, the suffering, and the human." Instead of inverting what they were (most likely they didn't have that choice), they deepened what they were. Their symbols disclose less contradiction and more "synthesis and paradox."

For women, courtship is an adventure in sprit, emotion, and physical expression.

213

And this doesn't end in "tying the knot" either. To the man, she has become the "ol' ball and chain". To the woman, it's time to go have fun and experience a new part of her life, with her partner.

A woman falls in love gradually and as takes a man into her emotions completely.

The man was physically attracted to the woman first; whereas, a woman is emotionally attracted to the man first. A woman marries based on a man's ability to get better. This term of "better" is important to a woman, but does not take the form of desiring to change the man, so much as, she expects him to grow and change within the relationship himself. In other words, as the relationship grows, he changes as the situation changes, not because of something the woman coerces or cajoles. The man understands status quo; the woman abhors the very thought of it. Women need to employ change gradually and progressively, at the same time, allowing men time to adjust and validate the change in their mind. This "validation" is not to be understood as a need to control the wife, but rather the need to understand what is happening.

Words Women Use

FINE

This is the word women use to end an argument when they feel they are right, and you need to shut up. Never use "fine" to describe how a woman looks - this will cause you to have one of those arguments.

FIVE MINUTES

This is half an hour. It is equivalent to the five minutes that your football game is going to last, before you take out the trash, so it's an even trade.

NOTHING

This means "something," and you should be on your toes. "Nothing" is usually used to describe the feeling a woman has of wanting to turn you inside out, upside down, and backwards. "Nothing" usually signifies an argument that will last "Five Minutes" and end with "Fine."

GO AHEAD (With Raised Eyebrows)

This is a dare. One that will result in a woman getting upset over "Nothing," and will end with the word "Fine."

GO AHEAD (Normal Eyebrows)

This means, "I give up," or "do what you want, because I don't care." You will get a "Raised Eyebrow Go Ahead" in just a few minutes, followed by "Nothing" and "Fine," and she will talk to you in about "Five Minutes" when she cools off.

LOUD SIGH

This is not actually a word, but is a nonverbal statement, often misunderstood by men. A "Loud Sigh" means she thinks you are an idiot at that moment, and wonders why she is wasting her time standing here, arguing with you over "Nothing".

SOFT SIGH

Again, this is not a word, but a nonverbal statement. "Soft Sighs" mean that she is content. Your best bet is to not move, or breathe, and she will stay content.

THAT'S OKAY

This is one of the most dangerous statements that a woman can make to a man. "That's Okay," means that she wants to think long and hard before paying you back for whatever it is that you have done. "That's Okay" is often used with the word "Fine," and in conjunction with a "Raised Eyebrow."

GO AHEAD

At some point in the near future, you are going to be in some mighty big trouble.

PLEASE DO

This is not a statement it is an offer. A woman is giving you the chance to come up with whatever excuse, or reason, you have for doing whatever it is that you have done. You have a fair chance with the truth, so be careful and you shouldn't get a "That's Okay."

THANKS

A woman is thanking you. Do not faint. Just say you're welcome.

THANKS A LOT

This is much different from "Thanks." A woman will say, "Thanks A Lot," when she is really ticked off at you. It signifies that you have offended her in some callous way, and will be followed by the "Loud Sigh." Be careful not to ask what is wrong after the "Loud Sigh," as she will only tell you "Nothing."

Chapter 3 – Key Danger Signs to Look For In Online Social Media Sites

In the previous two chapters, I gave you a good deal of information regarding the human mind. In Chapter 1, I laid a foundation of how the human mind operates and the actual "Mechanism of the Human Mind".

In Chapter 2, my goal and purpose was to demonstrate to you the differences in how each gender employs their respective psyches.

Now, in this Chapter 3, I am going to teach you criminal profiling and how to spot fraud artist simply by the words they use and how they structure their content.

*****

Gender-Sensitive Language
What is "gender-sensitive language" and why should I use it?

English speakers and writers have traditionally been taught to use masculine nouns and pronouns in situations where the gender of their subject(s) is unclear or variable, or when a group to which they are referring contains members of both sexes. For example, the U.S. Declaration of Independence states that " . . . all men are created equal . . ." and most of us were taught in elementary school to understand the word "men" in that context includes both male and female Americans. In recent decades, however, as women have become increasingly involved in the public sphere of American life, writers have reconsidered the way they express gender identities and relationships. Because most English language readers no longer understand the word "man" to be synonymous with "people," writers today must think more carefully about the ways they express gender in order to convey their ideas clearly and accurately to their readers.

NOTE: *This is important. Con artists write their content most often ignoring gender identity. They consistently use the word "man" to refer to both men and women.*

Moreover, these issues are important for people concerned about issues of social inequality. There is a relationship between our language use and our social reality. If we "erase" women from language, that makes it easier to maintain gender inequality. As Professor Sherryl Kleinman (2000:6) has argued,

[M]ale-based generics are another indicator—and, more importantly, a *reinforcer*—of a system in which "man" in the abstract and men in the flesh are privileged over women.

218

Words matter and our language choices have consequences. If we believe that women and men deserve social equality, then we should think seriously about how to reflect that belief in our language use.

You're probably already aware that tackling gender sensitivity in your writing is no small task, especially since there isn't yet (and there may never be) a set of concrete guidelines on which to base your decisions. Fortunately, there are a number of different strategies the gender-savvy writer can use to express gender relationships with precision.

Pronouns

A pronoun is a word that substitutes for a noun. The English language provides pronoun options for references to masculine nouns (for example, "he" can substitute for "Tom"), feminine nouns ("she" can replace "Lucy"), and neutral/non-human nouns ("it" stands in for "a tree"), but no choice for sex-neutral third-person singular nouns ("the writer," "a student," or "someone"). Although most of us learned in elementary school that masculine pronouns (he, his, him) should be used as the "default" in situations where the referent (that is, the person or thing to which you're referring) could be either male or female, that usage is generally considered unacceptable now. So what should you do when you're faced with one of those gender-neutral or gender-ambiguous situations? Well, you've got a few options:

1. Use "they"

This option is currently much debated by grammar experts, but most agree that it works well in at least several kinds of situations. In order to use "they" to express accurately gender relationships, you'll need to understand that "they" is traditionally used only to refer to a plural noun. For example,

Sojourner Truth and Elizabeth Cady Stanton were famous "first-wave" American feminists. *They* were also both involved in the Abolitionist movement.

In speech, though, we early twenty-first century Americans commonly use "they" to refer to a singular referent. According to many grammar experts, that usage is incorrect, but here's an example of how it sounds in our everyday speech:

If a student wants to learn more about gender inequality, they should take Intro to Women's Studies.

Note that in this example, "a student" is singular, but it is replaced in the second sentence by "they," a plural pronoun. In speech, we often don't notice such substitutions of the plural for the singular, but in writing, some will find such substitutions awkward or incorrect. Some people argue that "they" should become the default gender-neutral pronoun for English writing, but since that usage can still sound awkward to many readers, it's best to use "they" only in plural situations. Thus, one other option the gender-savvy writer may choose to employ is to make her/his sentence plural. Here's one way that can work:

A student's beliefs about feminism may be based on what **he** *has heard in the popular media...*can become...*Students' beliefs about feminism may be based on what* **they** *have heard in the popular media.*

2. Use she or he or she/he.

There is another, simpler option the gender-savvy writer can use to deal with situations where a pronoun needs to refer to a person whose gender isn't known: write out both pronoun options as "she or he" or "she/he." For example,

Each **student** *who majors in Women's Studies major must take a course in Feminist Theory.* **She or he** *may also get course credit for completing an internship at a local organization that benefits women.*

OR

Each **student** *who majors in Women's Studies major must take a course in Feminist Theory.* **She/he** *may also get course credit for completing an internship at a local organization that benefits women.*

3. Alternate genders and pronouns

You may also choose to alternate gendered pronouns. This option will work only in certain situations, though—usually hypothetical situations in which the referent is equally likely to be a male or a female. For example, both male and female students use the Writing Center's services, so the author of our staff manual chose to alternate between masculine and feminine pronouns when writing the following tutoring guidelines:

- Respond as a reader, explaining what and how you were/are thinking as you read her texts so that she can discover where a reader might struggle with her writing.
- Ask him to outline the draft to reveal the organization of the paper.
- Ask her to describe her purpose and audience and show how she has taken them into account in her writing.
- Explain a recurring pattern and let him locate repeated instances of it.

Of course, this author could also have included both pronouns in each sentence by writing "her/his" or "her/him," but in this case, alternating "he" and "she" conveys the same sense of gender variability and is likely a little easier on the reader, who won't have to pause to process several different options every time a gendered pronoun is needed in the sentence. This example also provides a useful demonstration of how gender-savvy writers can take advantage of the many different options available by choosing the one that best suits the unique requirements of each piece of writing they produce.

4. Eliminate the pronoun altogether

Finally, you can also simply eliminate the pronoun. For example,

Allan Johnson is a contemporary feminist theorist. This writer and professor gave a speech at UNC in the fall of 2007.

Note how the sentence used "this writer and professor" rather than "he."

*Many people accept the negative stereotype that if a person is a feminist, she must hate men...*could become...*Many people accept the negative stereotype that feminist beliefs are based on hatred of men.*

Note how the second version of the sentence talks about the beliefs. By avoiding using the pronoun "she," it leaves open the possibility that men may be feminists.

Gendered nouns

Like gendered pronouns, gendered nouns can also provide a stumbling block for the gender-savvy writer. The best way to avoid implications these words can carry is simply to be aware of how we tend to use them in speech and writing. Because gendered nouns are so commonly used and accepted by English writers and speakers, we often don't notice them or the implications they bring with them. Once you've recognized that a gender distinction is being made by such a word, though, conversion of the gendered noun into a gender-savvy one is usually very simple.

"Man" and words ending in "-man" are the most commonly used gendered nouns, so avoiding the confusion they bring can be as simple as watching out for these words and replacing them with words that convey your meaning more effectively. For example, if the founders of America had been gender-savvy writers, they might have written " . . . all people are created equal" instead of " . . . all men are created equal . . .."

Another common gendered expression, particularly in informal speech and writing, is "you guys." This expression is used to refer to groups of men, groups of women, and groups that include both men and women. Although most people *mean* to be inclusive when they use "you guys," this phrase wouldn't make sense if it didn't subsume women under the category "guys." To see why "you guys" is gendered male, consider that "a guy" (singular) is definitely a man, not a woman, and that most men would not feel included in the expression "you gals" or "you girls."

Another example of gendered language is the way the words "Mr.," "Miss," and "Mrs." are used. "Mr." can refer to any man, regardless of whether he is single or married—but women are defined by their relationship to men (by whether they are married or not). A way around this is to use "Ms." (which doesn't indicate marital status) to refer to women.

Sometimes we modify nouns that refer to jobs or positions to denote the sex of the person holding that position. This often done if the sex of the person holding the position goes against conventional expectations. To get a sense of these expectations, think about what sex you would instinctively assume the subject of each of these sentences to be:

The doctor walked into the room.

The nurse walked into the room.

Many people assume that doctors are men and that nurses are women. Because of such assumptions, someone might write sentences like "The female doctor walked into the room" or "The male nurse walked into the room." Using "female" and "male" in this way reinforces the assumption that most or all doctors are male and most or all nurses are female. Unless the sex of the nurse or doctor is important to the meaning of the sentence, it can be omitted.

As you work on becoming a gender-savvy writer, you may find it helpful to watch out for the following gendered nouns and replace them with one of the alternatives listed below. Check a thesaurus for alternatives to gendered nouns not included in this list.

gendered noun	gender-neutral noun
man	person, individual
freshman	first-year student
mankind	people, human beings, humanity
man-made	machine-made, synthetic
the common	the average (or ordinary) person

man	to operate, to cover, to staff
to man	chair, chairperson, coordinator
chairman	mail carrier, letter carrier, postal worker
mailman	police officer
policeman	flight attendant
steward, stewardess	congress person, legislator, representative
congressman	Dear Sir or Madam:, Dear Editor:, Dear Service Representative:, To Whom it May Concern:
Dear Sir:	

Proper nouns

Proper nouns can also give gender-savvy writers pause, but as with common nouns, it is usually very easy to use gender-neutral language once you've noticed the gendered patterns in your own writing. And the best way to avoid any confusion in your use of proper nouns is to use the same rules to discuss of women subjects as you already use when you're writing about men. In the examples below, notice how using different conventions for references to male and female subjects suggests a difference in the amount of respect being given to individuals on the basis of their gender.

1. Refer to women subjects by only their last names—just as you would do for men subjects.

226

For example, we would never refer to William Shakespeare as just "William;" we call him "Shakespeare" or "William Shakespeare." Thus, you should never refer to Jane Austen simply as "Jane;" you should write "Jane Austen" or "Austen."

2. In circumstances where you're writing about several people who have the same last name, try using the full name of the person every time you refer to him/her.

For example, if you're writing about George and Martha Washington, referring to him as "Washington" and her as "Martha" conveys a greater respect for him than for her. In order to express an equal amount of respect for these two historical figures, simply refer to each subject by her/his full name: "George Washington" and "Martha Washington." This option may sound like it could get too wordy, but it actually works very well in most situations.

3. Refer to women subjects by their full titles, just as you would refer to men subjects.

For example, you wouldn't call American President Reagan "Ronald," so you wouldn't want to refer to British Prime Minister Thatcher as "Margaret." Simply call her "Prime Minister Thatcher," just as you would write "President Reagan" to refer to him.

Sex versus gender

In many women's studies classes, one of the fundamental concepts students are expected to master is the difference feminists see between an individual's sex (which

227

feminists understand as one's biological makeup—male, female, or intersexed) and that person's gender (a social construction based on sex—man/masculine or woman/feminine). Because this distinction is so fundamental to understanding much of the material in many Women's Studies courses, expressing the difference between sex and gender is an important element in many writing assignments given by women's studies instructors.

Essentially, all you need to express sex vs. gender distinctions accurately in your writing is a clear understanding of the difference between sex and gender. As you are writing, ask yourself whether what you're talking about is someone's biological makeup or something about the way that person has been socialized. If you're referring to biology, use "male" or "female," and if what you're talking about has to do with a behavior or social role someone has been taught because of her/his biology, use "woman" or "man."

Thinking about the different answers to these two questions might help clarify the distinction between sex and gender:

What does it mean to be male?

What does it mean to be a man?

"To be male," as an expression of biological sex, is to have a chromosomal makeup of XY. "To be a man," however, expresses the socially constructed aspects of masculinity. Ideas of masculinity change across time, culture, and place. Think about the differences between what it meant "to be a man" in 17th-century France versus what it means "to be a man" today in the United States.

Checklist for gender revisions

To ensure that you've used gender savvy language in your piece of writing, try asking yourself the following questions:

1. Have you used "man" or "men" or words containing one of them to refer to people who may be female? If so, consider substituting another word. For example, instead of "fireman," try "firefighter."

2. If you have mentioned someone's gender, was it necessary to do so? If you identify someone as a female architect, for example, do you (or would you) refer to someone else as a "male architect"? And if you then note that the woman is an attractive blonde mother of two, do you mention that the man is a muscular, dark-haired father of three? Unless gender and related matters—looks, clothes, parenthood—are relevant to your point, leave them unmentioned.

3. Do you use any occupational stereotypes? Watch for the use of female pronouns for elementary school teachers and male ones for scientists, for example.

4. Do you use language that in any way shows a lack of respect for either sex?

5. Have you used "he," "him," "his," or "himself" to refer to people who may be female?

*****

I want to offer the following excellent article for your perusal. I have removed the figures and illustrations but have given you the article's URL so that you can read it online, which includes the credits too.

Personality, Gender, and Age in the Language of Social Media: The Open-Vocabulary Approach

- H. Andrew Schwartz mail,
- Johannes C. Eichstaedt,
- Margaret L. Kern,
- Lukasz Dziurzynski,
- Stephanie M. Ramones,
- Megha Agrawal,
- Achal Shah,
- Michal Kosinski,
- David Stillwell,
- Martin E. P. Seligman,
- Lyle H. Ungar

http://www.plosone.org/article/info%3Adoi%2F10.1371%2Fjournal.pone.0073791

Abstract

We analyzed 700 million words, phrases, and topic instances collected from the Facebook messages of 75,000 volunteers, who also took standard personality tests, and found striking variations in language with personality, gender, and age. In our *open-vocabulary* technique, the data itself drives a comprehensive exploration of language that distinguishes people, finding

230

connections that are not captured with traditional closed-vocabulary word-category analyses. Our analyses shed new light on psychosocial processes yielding results that are face valid (e.g., subjects living in high elevations talk about the mountains), tie in with other research (e.g., neurotic people disproportionately use the phrase 'sick of' and the word 'depressed'), suggest new hypotheses (e.g., an active life implies emotional stability), and give detailed insights (males use the possessive 'my' when mentioning their 'wife' or 'girlfriend' more often than females use 'my' with 'husband' or 'boyfriend'). To date, this represents the largest study, by an order of magnitude, of language and personality.

Citation: Schwartz HA, Eichstaedt JC, Kern ML, Dziurzynski L, Ramones SM, et al. (2013) Personality, Gender, and Age in the Language of Social Media: The Open-Vocabulary Approach. PLoS ONE 8(9): e73791. doi:10.1371/journal.pone.0073791

Editor: Tobias Preis, University of Warwick, United Kingdom

Received: January 23, 2013; **Accepted:** July 29, 2013; **Published:** September 25, 2013

Funding: Support for this research was provided by the Robert Wood Johnson Foundation's Pioneer Portfolio, through a grant to Martin Seligman, "Exploring Concept of Positive Health". The funders had no role in study design, data collection and analysis, decision to publish, or preparation of the manuscript.

Competing interests: The authors have declared that no competing interests exist.

Introduction

The social sciences have entered the age of data science, leveraging the unprecedented sources of written language that social media afford. Through media such as Facebook and Twitter, used regularly by more than $1/7^{th}$ of the world's population, variation in mood has been tracked diurnally and across seasons, used to predict the stock market, and leveraged to estimate happiness across time. Search patterns on Google detect influenza epidemics weeks before CDC data confirm them, and the digitization of books makes possible the quantitative tracking of cultural trends over decades. To make sense of the massive data available, multidisciplinary collaborations between fields such as computational linguistics and the social sciences are needed. Here, we demonstrate an instrument which uniquely describes similarities and differences among groups of people in terms of their differential language use.

Our technique leverages what people say in social media to find distinctive *words*, *phrases*, and *topics* as functions of known attributes of people such as gender, age, location, or psychological characteristics. The standard approach to correlating language use with individual attributes is to examine usage of *a priori* fixed sets of words, limiting findings to preconceived relationships with words or categories. In contrast, we extract a data-driven collection of *words*, *phrases*, and *topics*, in which the lexicon is based on the words of the text being analyzed. This yields a comprehensive description of the differences between groups of people for any given attribute, and allows one to find unexpected results. We call approaches like ours, which do not rely on *a priori* word or category judgments, *open-vocabulary* analyses.

We use *differential language analysis* (*DLA*), our particular method of open-vocabulary analysis, to find language features across millions of Facebook messages that distinguish demographic and psychological attributes. From a dataset of over 15.4 million Facebook messages collected from 75 thousand volunteers, we extract 700 million instances of *words*, *phrases*, and automatically generated *topics* and correlate them with gender, age, and personality. We replicate traditional language analyses by applying Linguistic Inquiry and Word Count (*LIWC*), a popular tool in psychology, to our data set. Then, we show that *open-vocabulary* analyses can yield additional *insights* (correlations between personality and behavior as manifest through language) and more *information* (as measured through predictive accuracy) than traditional *a priori* word-category approaches. We present a word cloud-based technique to visualize results of *DLA*. Our large set of correlations is made available for others to use (available at: http:www.wwbp.org/).

Background
This section outlines recent work linking language with personality, gender, and age. In line with the focus of this paper, we predominantly discuss works which sought to gain psychological *insights*. However, we also touch on

increasingly popular attempts at *predicting* personality from language in social media, which, for our study, offer an empirical means to compare a *closed vocabulary* analysis (relying on *a priori* word category human judgments) and an *open vocabulary* analysis (not relying on *a priori* word category judgments).

Personality refers to the traits and characteristics that make an individual unique. Although there are multiple ways to classify traits, we draw on the popular Five Factor Model (or "Big 5"), which classifies personality traits into five dimensions: *extraversion* (e.g., outgoing, talkative, active), *agreeableness* (e.g., trusting, kind, generous), *conscientiousness* (e.g., self-controlled, responsible, thorough), *neuroticism* (e.g., anxious, depressive, touchy), and *openness* (e.g., intellectual, artistic, insightful). With work beginning over 50 years ago and journals dedicated to it, the *FFM* is a well-accepted construct of personality.

Automatic Lexical Analysis of Personality, Gender, and Age
By examining what words people use, researchers have long sought a better understanding of human psychology. As Tauszczik & Pennebaker put it:

Language is the most common and reliable way for people to translate their internal thoughts and emotions into a form that others can understand. Words and language, then, are the very stuff of psychology and communication.

The typical approach to analyzing language involves counting word usage over pre-chosen categories of language. For example, one might place words like 'nose', 'bones', 'hips', 'skin', 'hands', and 'gut' into a *body* lexicon, and count how often words in the lexicon are used by *extraverts* or *introverts* in order to determine who talks about the body more. Of such word-category lexica, the most widely used is Linguistic Inquiry and Word Count or *LIWC*, developed over the last couple decades by human judges designating categories for common words. The 2007 version of *LIWC* includes 64 different categories of language ranging from part-of-speech (i.e. *articles*, *prepositions*, *past-tense verbs*, *numbers*,...) to topical categories (i.e. *family*, *cognitive mechanisms*, *affect*, *occupation*, *body*,...), as well as a few other attributes such as total number of words used.

Pennebaker & King conducted one of the first extensive applications of *LIWC* to personality by examining words in a variety of domains including diaries, college writing assignments, and social psychology manuscript abstracts. Their results were quite consistent across such domains, finding patterns such as *agreeable* people using more articles, *introverts* and those low in *conscientiousness* using more words signaling distinctions, and *neurotic* individuals using more negative emotion words. Mehl et al. tracks the natural speech of 96 people over two days. They found similar results to Pennebaker & King and that *neurotic* and *agreeable* people tend to use more first-person singulars, people low in *openness* talk more about social processes, *extraverts* use longer words.

235

The recent growth of online social media has yielded great sources of personal discourse. Besides advantages due to the size of the data, the content is often personal and describes everyday concerns. Furthermore, previous research has suggested populations for online studies and Facebook are quite representative. Sumner et al. examined the language of 537 Facebook users with *LIWC* while Holtgraves studied the text messages of 46 students. Findings from these studies largely confirmed past links with LIWC but also introduced some new links such as *neurotics* using more acronyms or those high in *openness* using more quotations.

The larger sample-sizes from social media also enabled the first study exploring personality as a function of single-word use. Yarkoni investigated LIWC categories along with single words in connection with Big-5 scores of 406 bloggers. He identified single word results which would not have been caught with *LIWC*, such as 'hug' correlating positively with *agreeableness* (there is no physical affection category in *LIWC*), but, considering the sparse nature of words, 406 blogs does not result in comprehensive view. For example, they find only 13 significant word correlations for *conscientiousness* while we find thousands even after Bonferonni-correcting significance levels. Additionally, they did not control for age or gender although they reported roughly 75% of their subjects were female. Still, as the most thorough point of comparison for *LIWC* results with personality,

Analogous to a personality construct, work has been done in psychology looking at the latent dimensions of self-expression. Chung and Pennebaker factor analyzed 119 adjectives used in student essays of "who you think you are" and discovered 7 latent dimensions labeled such as "sociability" or "negativity". They were able to relate these factors to the Big-5 and found only weak relations, suggesting 7 dimensions as an alternative construction. Later, Kramer and Chung ran the same method over 1000 unique words across Facebook status updates, finding three components labeled, "positive events", "informal speech", and "school". Although their vocabulary size was somewhat limited, we still see these as previous examples of open-vocabulary language analyses for psychology – no assumptions were made on the categories of words beyond part-of-speech.

LIWC has also been used extensively for studying gender and age. Many studies have focused on function words (articles, prepositions, conjunctions, and pronouns), finding females use more first-person singular pronouns, males use more articles, and that older individuals use more plural pronouns and future tense verbs. Other works have found males use more formal, affirmation, and informational words, while females use more social interaction, and deictic language. For age, the most salient findings include older individuals using more positive emotion and less negative emotion words, older individuals preferring fewer self-references (i.e. 'I', 'me') , , and stylistically there is less use of negation. Similar to our finding of 2000 topics (clusters of semantically-related words), Argamon et al. used factor analysis and identified 20 coherent components of word use to link gender and age, showing male components of language increase with age while female factors decrease.

Occasionally, studies find contradictory results. For example, multiple studies report that emoticons (i.e. ':)' ':-(') are used more often by females , , , but Huffaker & Calvert found males use them more in a sample of 100 teenage bloggers . This particular discrepancy could be sample-related – differing demographics or having a non-representative sample (Huffaker & Calvert looked at 100 bloggers, while later studies have looked at thousands of twitter users) or it could be due to differences in the domain of the text (blogs versus twitter). One should always be careful generalizing new results outside of the domain they were found as language is often dependent on context. In our case we explore language in the broad context of Facebook, and do not claim our results would up under other smaller or larger contexts. As a starting point for reviewing more psychologically meaningful language findings, we refer the reader to Tauszczik & Pennebaker's 2010 survey of computerized text analysis.

Eisenstein et al. presented a sophisticated *open-vocabulary* language analysis of demographics. Their method views language analysis as a multi-predictor to multi-output regression problem, and uses an L1 norm to select the most useful predictors (i.e. words). Part of their motivation was finding interpretable relationships between individual language features and sets of outcomes (demographics), and unlike the many predictive works we discuss in the next section, they test for significance of relationships between individual language features and outcomes. To contrast with our approach, we consider features and outcomes individually (i.e. an "L0 norm"), which we think is more ideal for our goals of explaining psychological variables (i.e. understanding openness by the words that correlate with it). For example, their method may throwout a word which is strongly predictive for only one outcome or which is collinear with other words, while we want to know all the words most-predictive for a given outcome. We also explore other types of *open-vocabulary* language features such as phrases and topics.

Similar language analyses also occurred in many fields outside of psychology or demographics. For example, Monroe et al. explored a variety of techniques that compare two frequencies of words – one number for each of two groups. In particular, they explored frequencies across democratic versus republican speeches and settled on a Bayesian model with regularization and shrinkage based on priors of word use. Lastly, Gilbert finds words and phrases that distinguish communication up or down a power-hierarchy across 2044 Enron emails. They used penalized logistic regression to fit a single model using coefficients of each feature as their "power"; this produces a good single predictive model but also means words which are highly collinear with others will be missed (we run a separate regression for each word to avoid this).

Perhaps one of the most comprehensive language analysis surveys outside of psychology is that of Grimmer & Stewart. They summarize how automated methods can inexpensively allow systematic analysis and inference from large political text collections, classifying types of analyses into a class of hierarchy. Additionally, they provide cautionary advice; In relation to this work, they note that dictionary methods (such as the closed-vocabulary analyses discussed here) may signal something different when used in a new domain (for example 'crude' may be a negative word in student essays, but be neutral in energy industry reports: 'crude oil'). For comprehensive surveys on text analyses across fields see Grimmer & Stewart, O'Connor, Bamman, & Smith, and Tausczik & Pennebaker.

Predictive Models based on Language
In contrast with the works seeking to gain *insights* about psychological variables, research focused on *predicting* outcomes have embraced data-driven approaches. Such work uses open-vocabulary linguistic features in addition to *a priori* lexicon based features in predictive models for tasks such as stylistics/authorship attribution –, emotion prediction , , interaction or flirting detection, or sentiment analysis. In other works, ideologies of political figures (i.e. conservative to liberal) have been predicted based on language using supervised techniques or unsupervised inference of ideological space. Sometimes these works note the highest weighted features, but with their goal being predictive accuracy, those features are not tested for significance and they usually are not the most individually distinguishing pieces of language. To elaborate, most approaches to prediction penalize the weights of words that are highly collinear with other words as they fit a single model per outcomes across all words. However, these highly collinear words which are suppressed could have revealed important insights with an outcome. In other words, these predictive models answer the question "what is the best combination of words and weights to predict personality?" whereas we believe answering the following question is best for

revealing new insights: "what words, controlled for gender and age, are individually most correlated with personality?"

Recently, researchers have started looking at personality prediction. Early works in personality prediction used dictionary-based features such as *LIWC*. Argamon et al. (2005) noted that personality, as detected by categorical word use, was supportive for author attribution. They examined language use according to the traits of *neuroticism* and *extraversion* over approximately 2200 student essays, while focused on using function words for the prediction of gender. Mairesse et al. used a variety of lexicon-based features to predict all Big-5 personality traits over approximately 2500 essays as well as 90 sets of individual spoken words. As a first pass at predicting personality from language in Facebook, Golbeck used *LIWC* features over a sample of 167 Facebook volunteers as well as profile information and found limited success of a regression model. Similarly, Kaggle held a competition of personality prediction over Twitter messages, providing participants with language cues based on *LIWC*. Results of the competition suggested personality is difficult to predict based on language in social media, but it is not clear whether such a conclusion would have been drawn had *open-vocabulary* language cues been supplied for prediction.

In the largest previous study of language and personality, Iacobelli, Gill, Nowson, and Oberlander attempted prediction of personality for 3,000 bloggers. Not limited to categorical language they found open-vocabulary features, such as bigrams, to be better predictors than

241

LIWC features. This motivates our exploration of open-vocabulary features for psychological insights, where we examine multi-word phrases (also called n-grams) as well as open-vocabulary category language in the form of automatically clustered groups of semantically related word (*LDA topics*, see "Linguistic Feature Extraction" in the "Materials and Methods" section). Since the application of Iacobelli's et al work was content customization, they focused on prediction rather than exploration of language for psychological insight. Our much larger sample size lends itself well to more comprehensive exploratory results.

Similar studies have also been undertaken for age and gender prediction in social media. Because gender and age information is more readily available, these studies tend to be larger. Argamon et al. predicted gender and age over 19,320 bloggers, while Burger et al. scaled up the gender prediction over 184,000 Twitter authors by using automatically guessed gender based-on gender-specific keywords in profiles. Most recently, Bamman et al. looked at gender as a function of language and social network statistics in twitter. They particularly looked at the characteristics of those whose gender was incorrectly predicted and found greater gender homophily in the social networks of such individuals.

These past studies, mostly within the field of computer science or specifically computational linguistics, have focused on prediction for tasks such as content personalization or authorship attribution. In our work, predictive models of personality, gender, and age provide a quantitative means to compare various *open-vocabulary* sets of features with a *closed-vocabulary* set. Our primary concern is to explore the benefits of an *open-vocabulary* approach for gaining *insights*, a goal that is at least as import as prediction for psychosocial fields. Most works for gaining language-based insights in psychology are *closed-vocabulary* (for examples, see previous section), and while many works in computational linguistics are open-vocabulary, they rarely focus on insight. We introduce the term "open-vocabulary" to distinguish an approach like ours from previous approaches to gaining *insight*, and in order to encourage others seeking insights to consider similar approaches. "Differential language analysis" refers to the particular process, for which we are not aware of another name, we use in our *open-vocabulary*.

Contributions

The contributions of this paper are as follows:

- First, we present the largest study of personality and language use to date. With just under 75,000 authors, our study covers an order-of-magnitude more people and instances of language features than the next largest study. The size of our data enables qualitatively different analyses, including open vocabulary analysis, based on more comprehensive sets of language features such as *phrases* and automatically derived *topics*. Most prior studies used *a priori* language categories, presumably due in part to the sparse nature of words and their relatively small samples of people. With smaller data sets, it is difficult to find statistically significant differences in language use for anything but the most common words.

- Our *open-vocabulary* analysis yields further insights into the behavioral residue of personality types beyond those from *a priori* word-category based approaches, giving unanticipated results (correlations between language and personality, gender, or age). For example, we make the novel discoveries that mentions of an assortment of social sports and life activities (such as *basketball*, *snowboarding*, *church*, *meetings*) correlate with *emotional stability*, and that *introverts* show an interest in Japanese media (such as *anime*, *pokemon*, *manga* and Japanese emoticons: ^_^). Our inclusion of phrases in addition to words provided further insights (e.g. that males prefer to precede 'girlfriend' or 'wife' with the possessive 'my' significantly more than females do for 'boyfriend' or 'husband'. Such correlations provide quantitative evidence for strong links between behavior, as revealed in language use, and psychosocial variables. In turn, these results suggest undertaking studies, such as directly measuring participation in activities in order to verify the link with emotional stability.

- We demonstrate open-vocabulary features contain more information than *a priori* word-categories via their use in predictive models. We take model accuracy in out-of-sample prediction as a measure of information of the features provided to the model. Models built from words and phrases as well as those from automatically generated topics achieve significantly higher out-of-sample prediction accuracies than standard lexica for each variable of interest (*gender*, *age*, and *personality*). Additionally, our prediction model for gender yielded state-of-the-art results for predictive models based entirely on language, yielding an out-of-sample accuracy of 91.9%.

- We present a word cloud visualization which scales words by correlation (i.e., how well they predict the given psychological variable) rather than simply scaling by frequency. Since we find thousands of significantly correlated words, visualization is key, and our *differential* word clouds provide a comprehensive view of our results.

- Lastly, we offer our comprehensive *word*, *phrase*, and *topic* correlation data for future research experiments (see: http://wwbp.org).

Materials and Methods
Ethics Statement
All research procedures were approved by the University of Pennsylvania Institutional Review Board. Volunteers agreed to written informed consent.

In seeking insights from language use about personality, gender, and age, we explore two approaches. The first approach, serving as a replication of the past analyses, counts word usage over manually created *a priori* word-category lexica. The second approach, termed *DLA*, serves as our main method and is *open-vocabulary* – the words and clusters of words analyzed are determined by the data itself.

Closed Vocabulary: Word-Category Lexica

A common method for linking language with psychological variables involves counting words belonging to manually-created categories of language. Sometimes referred to as the *word-count* approach, one counts how often words in a given category are used by an individual, the percentage of the participants' words which are from the given category:

$$p\ (category \mid subject) = \frac{\sum\limits_{word \in category} freq\ (word,\ subject)}{\sum\limits_{word \in vocab\ (subject)} freq\ (word,\ subject)}$$

where $freq\ (word, subject)$ is the number of the times the participant mentions $word$ and $vocab\ (subject)$ is the set of all words mentioned by the subject.

We use ordinary least squares regression to link word categories with author attributes, fitting a linear function between explanatory variables (*LIWC* categories) and dependent variables (such as a trait of personality, e.g. extraversion). The coefficient of the target explanatory variable (often referred to as β) is taken as the strength of relationship. Including other variables allows us to adjust for covariates such as gender and age to provide the unique effect of a given language feature on each psychosocial variable.

Open Vocabulary: Differential Language Analysis

Our technique, *differential language analysis* (*DLA*), is based on three key characteristics. It is

1. *Open-vocabulary* – it is not limited to predefined word lists. Rather, linguistic features including

words, phrases, and topics (sets of semantically related words) are automatically determined from the texts. (I.e., it is "data-driven".) This means *DLA* is classified as a type of open-vocabulary approach.

2. *Discriminating* – it finds key linguistic features that distinguish psychological and demographic attributes, using stringent significance tests.

3. *Simple* – it uses simple, fast, and readily accepted statistical techniques.

We depict the components of this approach, and describe the three steps: 1) linguistic feature extraction, 2) correlational analysis, and 3) visualization in the following sections.

1. Linguistic Feature Extraction

We examined two types of linguistic features: a) *words and phrases*, and b) *topics*. *Words and phrases* consisted of sequences of 1 to 3 words (often referred to as 'n-grams' of size 1 to 3). What constitutes a word is determined using a tokenizer, which splits sentences into tokens ("words"). We built an emoticon-aware tokenizer on top of Pott's "happyfuntokenizer" allowing us to capture emoticons like '<3' (a heart) or ':-)' (a smile), which most tokenizers incorrectly divide up as separate pieces of punctuation. When extracting phrases, we keep only those sequences of words with high informative value according to point wise mutual information (*PMI*) [69], [70], a ratio of the joint-probability to the independent probability of observing the phrase:

$$pmi\,(phrase) = \log \frac{p(phrase)}{\prod_{w \in phrase} p(w)}$$

In practice, we kept phrases with pmi values greater than $2 * length$, where $length$ is the number of words contained in the phrase, ensuring that phrases we do keep are informative parts of speech and not just accidental juxtapositions. All word and phrase counts are normalized by each subject's total word use ($p(word \mid subject)$), and we apply the Anscombe transformation to the normalized values for variance stabilization (P_{ans}):

$$p(phrase \mid subject) = \frac{freq\,(phrase,\,subject)}{\sum_{phrase' \in vocab(subject)} freq\,(phrase',\,subject)}$$

$$p_{ans}(phrase \mid subject) = 2\sqrt{p(phrase \mid subject) + 3/8}$$

where $vocab(subject)$ returns a list of all words and phrases used by that subject. These Anscombe transformed "relative frequencies" of words or phrases (P_{Ans}) are then used as the independent variables in all our analyses. Lastly, we restrict our analysis to those words and phrases which are used by at least 1% of our subjects, keeping the focus on common language.

The second type of linguistic feature, *topics*, consists of word clusters created using Latent Dirichlet Allocation (LDA). The LDA generative model assumes that documents (i.e. Facebook messages) contain a combination of topics, and that topics are a distribution of words; since the words in a document are known, the latent variable of topics can be estimated through Gibbs sampling. We use an implementation of the LDA algorithm provided by the Mallet package, adjusting one parameter ($alpha = 0.30$) to favor fewer topics per document, since individual Facebook status updates tend to contain fewer topics than the typical documents (newspaper or encyclopedia articles) to which LDA is applied. All other parameters were kept at their default. An example of such a model is the following sets of words (*tuesday, monday, wednesday, friday, thursday, week, sunday, saturday*) which clusters together days of the week purely by exploiting their similar distributional properties across messages.

To use topics as features, we find the probability of a subject's use of each *topic*:

$$p(topic \mid subject) = \sum_{word \in topic} p(topic \mid word) * p(word \mid subject)$$

where $p(word \mid subject)$ is the normalized word use by that subject and $p(topic \mid word)$ is the probability of the topic given the word (a value provided from the LDA procedure). The prevalence of a word in a topic is given by $p(topic, word)$, and is used to order the words within a topic when displayed.

2. Correlational Analysis

Similar to word categories, distinguishing open-vocabulary words, phrases, and topics can be identified using ordinary least squares regression. We again take the coefficient of the target explanatory variable as its correlation strength, and we include other variables (e.g. age and gender) as covariates to get the unique effect of the target explanatory variable. Since we explore many features at once, we consider coefficients significant if they are less than a Bonferroni-corrected two-tailed p of

249

0.001. (I.e., when examining 20,000 features, a passing p-value is less than 0.001 divided by 20,000 which is $5 * 10^{-8}$).

Our correlational analysis produces a comprehensive list of the most distinguishing language features for any given attribute, *words, phrases,* or *topics* which maximally discriminate a given target variables. For example, when we correlate the target variables geographic elevation with language features ($N = 18,383$, $p < 0.001$, adjusted for gender and age), we find 'beach' the most distinguishing feature for low elevation localities, and 'the mountains' to be among the most distinguishing features for high elevation localities, (i.e., people in low elevations talk about the beach more, whereas people at high elevations talk about the mountains more). Similarly, we find the most distinguishing topics to be *(beach, sand, sun, water, waves, ocean, surf, sea, toes, sandy, surfing, beaches, sunset, Florida, Virginia)* for low elevations and *(Colorado, heading, headed, leaving, Denver, Kansas, City, Springs, Oklahoma, trip, moving, Iowa, KC, Utah, bound)* for high elevations. Others have looked at geographic location.

3. Visualization

An analysis over tens of thousands of language features and multiple dimensions results in hundreds of thousands of statistically significant correlations. Visualization is thus critical for their interpretation. We use word clouds to intuitively summarize our results. Unlike most word clouds, which scale word size by their frequency, we scale word size according to the strength of the correlation of the word with the demographic or psychological measurement of interest, and we use color to represent frequency over all subjects; that is, larger words indicate stronger correlations, and darker colors indicate more frequently used words. This provides a clear picture of which words and phrases are most discriminating while not losing track of which ones are the most frequent. Word clouds scaled by frequency are often used to summarize news, a practice that has been critiqued for inaccurately representing articles. Here, we believe the word cloud is an appropriate visualization because the individual words and phrases we depict in it are the actual results we wish to summarize. Further, scaling by correlation coefficient rather than frequency gives clouds that distinguish a given outcome.

Word clouds can also used to represent distinguishing topics. In this case, the size of the word within the topic represents its prevalence among the cluster of words making up the topic. We use the 6 most distinguishing topics and place them on the perimeter of the word clouds for *words and phrases*. This way, a single figure gives a comprehensive view of the most distinguishing words, phrases, and topics for any given variables of interest.

To reduce the redundancy of results, we automatically prune language features containing information already provided by a feature with higher correlation. First, we sort language features in order of their correlation with a target variable (such as a personality trait). Then, for phrases, we use frequency as a proxy for informative value, and only include additional phrases if they contain more informative words than previously included phrases with matching words. For example, consider the phrases 'day', 'beautiful day', and 'the day', listed in order of correlation from greatest to least; 'Beautiful day' would be kept, because 'beautiful' is less frequent than 'day' (i.e., it is adding informative value), while 'the day' would be dropped because 'the' is more frequent than 'day' (thus it is not contributing more information than we get from 'day'). We do a similar pruning for topics: A lower-ranking topic is not displayed if more than 25% of its top 15 words are also contained in the top 15 words of a higher ranking topic. These discarded relationships are still statistically significant, but removing them provides more room in the visualizations for other significant results, making the visualization as a whole more meaningful.

Word clouds allow one to easily view the features most correlated with polar outcomes; we use other visualizations to display the variation of correlation of language features with continuous or ordinal dependent variables such as age. A standard time-series plot works well, where the horizontal axis is the dependent variable and the vertical axis represents the standard score of the values produced from feature extraction. When plotting language as a function of age, we fit first-order LOESS regression lines to the age as the x-axis data and standardized frequency as the y-axis data over all users. We are able to adjust for gender in the regression model by including it as a covariate when training the LOESS model and then using a neutral gender value when plotting.

Data Set: Facebook Status Updates

Our complete dataset consists of approximately 19 million Facebook status updates written by 136,000 participants. Participants volunteered to share their status updates as part of the *My Personality* application, where they also took a variety of questionnaires. We restrict our analysis to those Facebook users meeting certain criteria: They must indicate English as a primary language, have written at least 1,000 words in their status updates, be less than 65 years (to avoid the non-representative sample above 65), and indicate both gender and age (for use as controls). This resulted in $N = 74,941$ volunteers, writing a total of 309 million words (700 million feature instances of words, phrases, and topics) across 15.4 million status updates. From this sample each person wrote an average of 4,129 words over 206 status updates, and thus 20 words per update. Depending on the target variable, this number slightly varies as indicated in the caption of each result.

The personality scores are based on the International Personality Item Pool proxy for the NEO Personality Inventory Revised (NEO-PI-R). Participants could take 20 to 100 item versions of the questionnaire, with a retest reliability of $\alpha > 0.80$. With the addition of gender and age variables, this resulted in seven total dependent variables studied in this work. Personality distributions are quite typical with means near zero and standard deviations near 1. The statuses ranged over 34 months, from January 2009 through October 2011. Previously, profile information (i.e. network metrics, relationship status) from users in this dataset have been linked with personality, but this is the first use of its status updates.

Results

Results of our analyses over gender, age, and personality are presented below. As a baseline, we first replicate the commonly used *LIWC* analysis on our data set. We then present our main results, the output of our method, *DLA*. Lastly, we explore empirical evidence that *open-vocabulary* features provide more information than those from an *a priori* lexicon through use in a predictive model.

Closed Vocabulary

<u>Figure 2</u> shows the results of applying the *LIWC* lexicon to our dataset, along side-by-side with the most comprehensive previous studies we could find for *gender*, *age*. and *personality*. In our case, correlation results are βvalues from an ordinary least squares linear regression where we can adjust for gender and age to give the unique effect of the target variable. One should keep in mind that it is often found that effect sizes tend to be relatively smaller as sample sizes increase and become more stable.

Even though the previous studies listed did not look at Facebook, a majority of the correlations we find agree in direction. Some of the largest correlations emerge for the LIWC *articles* category, which consists of determiners like 'the', 'a', 'an' and serves as a proxy for the use of more nouns. Articles are highly predictive of males, being older, and *openness*. As a content-related language variable, the *anger* category also proved highly predictive for *males* as well as younger individuals, those low in *agreeableness* and *conscientiousness*, and high in *neuroticism. Openness* had the least agreement with the comparison study; roughly half of our results were in the opposite direction from the prior work. This is not too surprising since *openness* exhibits the most variation across conditions of other studies (for examples, see), and its component traits are most loosely related.

Open Vocabulary
Our *DLA* method identifies the most distinguishing language features (*words, phrases*: a sequence of 1 to 3 words, or *topics*: a cluster of semantically related words) for any given attribute. Results progress from a one variable proof of concept (gender), to the multiple variables representing age groups, and finally to all 5 dimensions of personality.
Language of Gender.

Gender provides a familiar and easy to understand proof of concept for open-vocabulary analysis. Figure 3 presents word clouds from age-adjusted gender correlations. We scale word size according to the strength of the relation and we use color to represent overall frequency; that is, larger words indicate stronger correlations, and darker colors indicate frequently used words. For the *topics*, groups of semantically-related words, the size indicate the relative prevalence of the word within the cluster as defined in the methods section. All results are significant at Bonferroni-corrected $p < 0.001$.

Many strong results emerging from our analysis align with our *LIWC* results and past studies of gender. For example, females used more emotion words (e.g., 'excited'), and first-person singulars, and they mention more psychological and social processes (e.g., 'love you' and ' <3' –a heart). Males used more swear words, object references (e.g., 'xbox' and swear words).

Other results of ours contradicted past studies, which were based upon significantly smaller sample sizes than ours. For example, in 100 bloggers Huffaker et al. found males use more emoticons than females. We calculated power analyses to determine the sample size needed to confidently find such significant results. Since the Bonferonni-correction we use elsewhere in this work is overly stringent (i.e. makes it harder than necessary to pass significance tests), for this result we applied the Benjamini-Hochberg false discovery rate procedure for multiple hypothesis testing. Rerunning our language of gender analysis on reduced random samples of our subjects resulted in the following number of significant correlations (Benjamini-Hochberg tested $p < 0.001$): 50 subjects: 0 significant correlations, 500 subjects: 7 correlations; 5,000 subjects: 1,489 correlations; 50,000 subjects: 13,152 correlations (more detailed results of power analyses across gender, age, and personality can be found in Figure S1). Thus, traditional study sample sizes, which are closer to 50 or 500, are not powerful enough to do data-driven DLA over individual words.

One might also draw insights based on the gender results. For example, we noticed 'my wife' and 'my girlfriend' emerged as strongly correlated in the male results, while simply 'husband' and 'boyfriend' were most predictive for females. Investigating the frequency data revealed that males did in fact precede such references to their opposite-sex partner with 'my' significantly more often than females. On the other hand, females were more likely to precede 'husband' or 'boyfriend' with 'her' or 'amazing' and a greater variety of words, which is why 'my husband' was not more predictive than 'husband' alone. Furthermore, this suggests the male preference for the possessive 'my' is at least partially due to a lack of talking about others' partners.

Language of Age

Figure 4 shows the word cloud (center) and most discriminating topics (surrounding) for four age buckets chosen with regard to the distribution of ages in our sample (Facebook has many more young people). We see clear distinctions, such as use of slang, emoticons, and Internet speak in the youngest group (e.g. ':)', 'idk', and a couple *Internet speak* topics) or work appearing in the 23 to 29 age group (e.g. 'at work', 'new job', as a *job position* topic). We also find subtle changes of topics progressing from one age group to the next. For example, we see a *school* related topic for 13 to 18 year olds (e.g. 'school', 'homework', 'ugh'), while we see a *college* related topic for 19 to 22 year olds (e.g. 'semester', 'college', 'register'). Additionally, consider the *drunk* topic (e.g. 'drunk', 'hangover', 'wasted') that appears for 19 to 22 year olds and a more reserved *beer* topic (e.g. 'beer', 'drinking', 'ale') for 23 to 29 year olds.

In general, we find a progression of school, college, work, and family when looking at the predominant topics across all age groups. *DLA* may be valuable for the generation of hypotheses about life span developmental age differences. Figure 5A shows the relative frequency of the most discriminating topic for each age group as a function of age. Typical concerns peak at different ages, with the topic concerning relationships (e.g. 'son', 'daughter', 'father', 'mother') continuously increasing across life span. On a similar note, Figure 5C shows 'we' increases approximately linearly after the age of 22, whereas 'I' monotonically decreases. We take this as a proxy for social integration, suggesting the increasing importance of friendships and relationships as people age. Figure 5B reinforces this hypothesis by presenting a similar pattern based on other social topics. One limitation of our dataset is the rarity of older individuals using social media; we look forward to a time in which we can track fine-grained language differences across the entire lifespan.

A. Standardized frequency for the best topic for each of the 4 age groups. Grey vertical lines divide groups: 13 to 18 (black: $n = 25,467$ out of $N = 74,859$), 19 to 22 (green: $n = 21,687$), 23 to 29 (blue: $n = 14,656$), and 30+ (red: $n = 13,049$). Lines are fit from first-order LOESS regression controlled for gender. **B**. Standardized frequency of social topic use across age. **C**. Standardized 'I', 'we' frequencies across age.

Language of Personality
We created age and gender-adjusted word clouds for each personality factor based on around 72 thousand participants with at least 1,000 words across their Facebook status updates, who took a Big Five questionnaire.

Figure 6 shows word clouds for extraversion and neuroticism. (See Figure S2 for openness, conscientiousness, and agreeableness.) The dominant words in each cluster were consistent with prior lexical and questionnaire work. For example, extraverts were more likely to mention social words such as 'party', 'love you', 'boys', and 'ladies', whereas introverts were more likely to mention words related to solitary activities such as 'computer', 'Internet', and 'reading'. In the openness cloud, words such as 'music', 'art', and 'writing' (i.e., creativity), and 'dream', 'universe', and 'soul' (i.e., imagination) were discriminating.

Topics were also found reflecting similar concepts as the words, some of which would not have been captured with *LIWC*. For example, although *LIWC* has socially related categories, it does not contain a *party* topic, which emerges as a key distinguishing feature for extraverts. Topics related to other types of social events are listed elsewhere, such as a sports topic for low neuroticism (emotional stability). Additionally, Figure 6 shows the advantage of having phrases in the analysis to get clearer signal: e.g. people high in neuroticism mentioned 'sick of', and not just 'sick'.

While many of our results confirm previous research, demonstrating the instrument's face validity, our word clouds also suggest new hypotheses. For example, Figure 6 (bottom-right) shows language related to emotional stability (low neuroticism). Emotionally stable individuals wrote about enjoyable social activities that may foster greater emotional stability, such as 'sports', 'vacation', 'beach', 'church', 'team', and a *family time* topic. Additionally, results suggest that introverts are interested in Japanese media (e.g. 'anime', 'manga', 'japanese', Japanese style emoticons: ^_^, and an *anime* topic) and that those low in *openness* drive the use of shorthands in social media (e.g. '2day', 'ur', 'every 1'). Although these are only language correlations, they show how *open-vocabulary* analyses can illuminate areas to explore further.

Predictive Evaluation
Here we present a quantitative evaluation of open-vocabulary and closed vocabulary language features. Although we have thus far presented subjective evidence that open-vocabulary features contribute more information, we hypothesize empirically that the inclusion of open-vocabulary features leads to prediction accuracies above and beyond that of closed-vocabulary. We randomly sampled 25% of our participants as test data, and used the remaining 75% as training data to build our predictive models.

We use a linear support vector machine (*SVM*) for classifying the binary variable of gender, and ridge regression for predicting age and each factor of personality. Features were first run through principal component analysis to reduce the feature dimension to half of the number of users. Both SVM classification and ridge regression utilize a regularization parameter, which we set by validation over the training set (we defined a small validation set of 10% of the training set which we tested various regularization parameters over while fitting the model to the other 90% of the training set in order to select the best parameter). Thus, the predictive model is created without any outcome information outside of the training data, making the test data an out-of-sample evaluation.

As open-vocabulary features, we use the same units of language as *DLA*: *words and phrases* (n-grams of size 1 to 3, passing a collocation filter) and *topics*. These features are outlined precisely under the "Linguistic Feature Extraction" section presented earlier. As explained in that section, we use Anscombe transformed relative frequencies of *words and phrases* and the conditional probability of a *topic* given a subject. For closed vocabulary features, we use the *LIWC* categories of language calculated as the relative frequency of a user mentioning a word in the category given their total word usage. We do not provide our models with anything other than these language usage features (independent variables) for prediction, and we use usage of all features (not just those passing significance tests from *DLA*).

As shown in Table 2, we see that models created with *open vocabulary* features significantly ($p < 0.01$) outperformed those created based on *LIWC* features. The *topics* results are of particular interest, because these automatically clustered word-category lexica were not created with any human or psychological data – only knowing what words occurred in messages together. Furthermore, we see that a model which includes *LIWC* features on top of the *open-vocabulary words*, *phrases*, and *topics* does not result in any improvement suggesting that the open-vocabulary features are able to capture predictive information which fully supersedes *LIWC*.

For personality we saw the largest relative improvement between *open-vocabulary* approaches and *LIWC*. Our best personality Rscore of 0.42 fell just above the standard "correlational upper-limit" for behavior to predict personality (a Pearson correlation of 0.3 to 0.4). Some researchers have discretized the personality scores for prediction, and classified people as being high or low (one standard deviation above or below the mean or top and bottom quartiles, throwing out the middle) in each trait. When we do such an approach, our scores are in similar ranges to such literature: 65% to 79% classification accuracy. Of course, such a high/low model cannot directly be used for classifying unlabeled people as one would also need to know who fits in the middle. Regression is a more appropriate predictive task for continuous outcomes like age and personality, even though Rscores are naturally smaller than binary classification accuracies.

We ran additional tests to evaluate only those words and phrases, topics, or *LIWC* categories that are selected via differential language analysis rather than all features. Thus, we used only those language features that significantly correlated (Bonferonni-corrected $p < 0.001$) with the outcome being predicting. To keep consistent with the main evaluation, we used no controls, and so one could view this as a univariate feature selection over each type of feature independently. We again found significant improvement from using the open-vocabulary features over *LIWC* and no significant changes in accuracy overall. These results are presented in Table S2.

In addition to demonstrating the greater informative value of *open-vocabulary* features, we found our results to be state-of-the-art. The highest previous *out-of-sample* accuracies for gender prediction based *entirely* on language were 88.0% over twitter data while our classifiers reach an accuracy of *91.9%*. Our increased performance could be attributed to our set of language features, a strong predictive algorithm (the support vector machine), and the large sample of Facebook data.

Discussion

Online social media such as Facebook are a particularly promising resource for the study of people, as "status" updates are self-descriptive, personal, and have emotional content. Language use is objective and quantifiable behavioral data, and unlike surveys and questionnaires, Facebook language allows researchers to observe individuals as they freely present themselves in their own words. *Differential language analysis* (*DLA*) in social media is an unobtrusive and non-reactive window into the social and psychological characteristics of people's everyday concerns.

Most studies linking language with psychological variables rely on *a priori* fixed sets of words, such as the *LIWC* categories carefully constructed over 20 years of human research. Here, we show the benefits of an *open-vocabulary* approach in which the words analyzed are based on the data itself. We extracted *words*, *phrases*, and *topics* (automatically clustered sets of words) from millions of Facebook messages and found the language that correlates most with gender, age, and five factors of personality. We discovered insights not found previously and achieved higher accuracies than *LIWC* when using our *open-vocabulary* features in a predictive model, achieving state-of-the-art accuracy in the case of gender prediction.

Exploratory analyses like *DLA* change the process from that of testing theories with observations to that of data-driven identification of new connections. Our intention here is not a complete replacement for *closed-vocabulary* analyses like *LIWC*. When one has a specific theory in mind or a small sample size, an *a priori* list of words can be ideal; in an open-vocabulary approach, the concept one cares about can be drowned out by more predictive concepts. Further, it may be easier to compare static *a priori* categories of words across studies. However, automatically clustering words into coherent topics allows one to potentially discover categories that might not have been anticipated (e.g. sports teams, kinds of outdoor exercise, or Japanese cartoons). Open-vocabulary approaches also save labor in creating categories. They consider all words encountered and thus are able to adapt well to the evolving language in social media or other genres. They are also transparent in that the exact words driving correlations are not hidden behind a level of abstraction. Given lots of text and dependent variables, an open-vocabulary approach like *DLA* can be immediately useful for many areas of study; for example, an economist contrasting sport utility with hybrid vehicle drivers, a political scientist comparing democrats and republicans, or a cardiologist differentiating people with positive versus negative outcomes of heart disease.

Like most studies in the social sciences, this work is still subject to sampling and social desirability biases. Language connections with psychosocial variables are often dependent on context. Here, we examined language in a large sample of the broad context of Facebook. Under different contexts, it is likely some results would differ. Still, the sample sizes and availability of demographic information afforded by social media bring us closer to a more ideal representative sample. Our current results have face validity (subjects in high elevations talk about 'the mountains'), tie in with other research (neurotic people disproportionately use the phrase 'depressed'), suggest new hypotheses (an active life implies emotional stability), and give detailed insights (males prefer to precede 'wife' with the possessive 'my' more so than females precede 'husband' with 'my').

Over the past one-hundred years, surveys and questionnaires have illuminated our understanding of people. We suggest that new multipurpose instruments such as *DLA* emerging from the field of computational social science shed new light on psychosocial phenomena.

*****

Criminal profiling is more often known as "offender profiling" within law enforcement circles. I want to include an article from Wikipedia that is actually quite good.

Offender Profiling

Offender profiling, also known as **criminal profiling**, is a behavioral and investigative tool that is intended to help investigators to accurately predict and profile the characteristics of unknown criminal subjects or offenders. Offender profiling is also known as criminal profiling, criminal personality profiling, criminological profiling, behavioral profiling or criminal investigative analysis. Geographic profiling is another method to profile an offender. Television shows such as *Law & Order: Criminal Intent*, *Profiler* in the 1990s, the 2005 television series *Criminal Minds*, the 2011 one season television series *Criminal Minds: Suspect Behavior*, and the 1991 film *The Silence of the Lambs* have lent many names to what the FBI calls "criminal investigative analysis." Or the BAU (Criminal Minds)

Holmes and Holmes (2008) outline the three main goals of criminal profiling:

- The first is to provide law enforcement with a social and psychological assessment of the offender;
- The second goal is to provide law enforcement with a "psychological evaluation of belongings found in the possession of the offender" (p. 10);
- The third goal is to give suggestions and strategies for the interviewing process.

Ainsworth (2001) identified that there are four main approaches to offender profiling:

266

- The geographical approach, in which the patterns are analyzed in regard to timing and location of the crime scene, in order to determine where the offender lives and works
- Investigative psychology, this approach focuses on the use of psychological theories of analysis to determine the characteristics of the offender by looking at the presented offending behavior and style of offense
- The typological approach looks at the specific characteristics of the crime scene to then categorize the offender according to the various 'typical' characteristics
- The clinical approach to offender profiling in which the understanding of psychiatry and clinical psychology is used to determine whether the offender is suffering from mental illness of various psychological abnormalities.

5 Procedural steps in generating a profile:

- 1. A thorough analysis of the type/nature of the criminal act is made and it is then compared to the types of people who have committed similar crimes in the past
- 2. An in depth analysis of the actual crime scene is made
- 3. The victim's background and activities are analyzed, to look for possible motives and connections

- 4. The possible factors for the motivation of the crime are analyzed
- 5. The description of the possible offender is developed, founded on the detected characteristics, which can be compared to with previous cases

In modern criminology, offender profiling is generally considered the "third wave" of investigative science:

- the first wave was the study of clues, pioneered by Scotland Yard in the 19th century;
- the second wave was the study of crime itself (frequency studies and the like);
- this third wave is the study of the psyche of the criminal.

Definitions

Offender profiling is a method of identifying the perpetrator of a crime based on an analysis of the nature of the offense and the manner in which it was committed. Various aspects of the criminal's personality makeup are determined from his or her choices before, during, and after the crime. This information is combined with other relevant details and physical evidence, and then compared with the characteristics of known personality types and mental abnormalities to develop a practical working description of the offender.

Psychological profiling may be described as a method of suspect identification which seeks to identify a person's mental, emotional, and personality characteristics (as manifested in things done or left at the crime scene). This was used in the investigation of the serial murders committed by Ted Bundy. Dr. Richard B. Jarvis, a psychiatrist with expertise on the criminal mind, predicted the age range of Bundy, his sexual psychopathy, and his above average intellect.

A further, more detailed example of how psychological profiling may be performed is the investigation of Gary Leon Ridgway, also known as the Green River Killer. This case also demonstrates the potential for incorrect predictions. John E. Douglas, an investigator who worked for the FBI, provided a twelve-page profile, which stated the suspect was:

- Probably a white male who had a dysfunctional relationship with women.
- Organized since he tried to hide the bodies and appeared to spend some time at the river
- Cunning in using rocks to weigh the victims down in the water to conceal them.
- Very mobile with a vehicle.
- Going to kill again.
- Like other serial killers, he would be prone to contacting police wanting to help in the investigations.

However, the profile created for Ridgway also revealed characteristics that did not apply to him, such as being an outdoorsman and being incapable of closeness to other people. Ridgway was not an outdoorsman, but frequented the Green River with one of his wives, and also had a very close relationship with his last wife, which

269

contradicted the point in the profile of being incapable of closeness.

One type of criminal profiling is referred to as linkage analysis. Gerard N. Labuschagne (2006) defines linkage analysis as "a form of behavioral analysis that is used to determine the possibility of a series of crimes as having been committed by one offender." Gathering many aspects of the offender's crime pattern such as modus operandi, ritual or fantasy-based behaviors exhibited, and the signature of the offender help to establish a basis for a linkage analysis. An offender's modus operandi is his or her habits or tendencies during the killing of the victim. An offender's signature is the unique similarities in each of his or her kills. Mainly, linkage analysis is used when physical evidence, such as DNA, cannot be collected.

Labuschagne states that in gathering and incorporating these aspects of the offender's crime pattern, investigators must engage in five assessment procedures: (1) obtaining data from multiple sources; (2) reviewing the data and identifying significant features of each crime across the series; (3) classifying the significant features as either MO and/or ritualistic; (4) comparing the combination of MO and ritual/fantasy-based features across the series to determine if a signature exists; and (5) compiling a written report highlighting the findings.

History

The origins of profiling can be traced back to as early as the Middle Ages, with the inquisitors trying to "profile" heretics. Jacob Fries, Cesare Lombroso, Alphonse

Bertillon, Hans Gross and several others realized the potential of profiling in the 19th century although their research is generally considered to be prejudiced, reflecting the biases of their time.

In 1912, a psychologist in Lackawanna, New York delivered in lecture in which he analyzed an unknown criminal who was suspected of having murdered a local boy named Joey Joseph. Based on the postcards which had been used to taunt the Lackawanna Police and the Joseph family, the profile ultimately led to the arrest and conviction of J. Frank Hickey.

A version of profiling is thought to have been used in the 1940s, when investigations relied on mental health professionals to create a profile of an offender in order to aid the police investigation. Soon after, as discussed below, James Brussel was called upon to analyze the information on the Mad Bomber in New York City, and he created an accurate profile of the offender. This caught the attention of the FBI, who then worked to develop a technique for profiling, based on the process used by Brussel.

Notable profilers

Thomas Bond

During the 1880s, Thomas Bond, a medical doctor, tried to profile the personality of Jack the Ripper. Bond, a police surgeon, assisted in the autopsy of Mary Kelly. In his notes, dated November 10, 1888, he mentioned the sexual nature of the murders coupled with elements of apparent misogyny and rage. Dr. Bond also tried to reconstruct the murder and interpret the behavior pattern of the offender: soon he came up with a profile or signature personality traits of the offender to assist police investigation. The profile said that five murders of seven in the area at the time the report was written had been committed by one person alone who was physically strong, composed, and daring. The unknown offender would be quiet and harmless in appearance, possibly middle-aged, and neatly attired, probably wearing a cloak to hide the bloody effects of his attacks out in the open. He would be a loner, without a real occupation, eccentric, and mentally unstable. He might even suffer from a condition called Satyriasis, a sexual deviancy that is today referred to as hypersexuality or promiscuity. Bond also mentioned that he believed the offender had no anatomical knowledge and could not be a surgeon or butcher. Moreover, Dr. Bond later concluded that the same offender was responsible for the murder of Alice McKenzie.

- Example of what Dr. Thomas Bond's First Profile of Jack the Ripper was:

"The murderer must have been a man of physical strength and great coolness and daring…subject to periodic attacks of homicidal and erotic mania. The characters of the mutilations indicate that the man may be in a condition sexually, that may be called Satyriasis"

Walter C. Langer

272

In 1943, Major General William J. Donovan, chief of the US Office of Strategic Services (OSS), asked Dr. Walter C. Langer, a psychoanalyst based in Boston, to develop a "profile" of Adolf Hitler. What the OSS wanted was a behavioral and psychological analysis of how Hitler might behave if the war turned against him.

Dr. Langer used speeches, Hitler's book Mein Kampf, interviews with people who had known Hitler, and some four hundred published works to complete his wartime report, which was eventually declassified by OSS and published by Langer (along with certain collateral material) as The Mind of Adolf Hitler in 1972. This work contains a profile of possible behavioral traits of Hitler, and his possible reactions to the idea of Germany losing World War II. Dr. Langer's profile noted that Hitler was meticulous, conventional, and prudish about his appearance and body. He was robust and viewed himself as a standard-bearer and trendsetter. He had manic phases, yet took little exercise. Due to a lack of evidence, Langer believed that Hitler was in reasonably good health, so it was unlikely he would die from natural causes, but he was deteriorating mentally. He would not try to escape to a neutral country, nor would he (in Langer's opinion) allow himself to be captured by the Allies. Hitler always walked diagonally from one corner to another when crossing a room, and he whistled a marching tune. He feared syphilis and germs.

Langer's profile also pointed out Hitler's oedipal complex, with the effect being the need to prove his manhood to his mother, and his masochistic coprolagnia and urolagnia. He detested the learned and the privileged, but enjoyed classical music, vaudeville, and Richard Wagner's opera. He showed strong streaks of sadism and liked circus acts that were risky and dangerous. He tended to speak in long monologues rather than have conversations. He had difficulty establishing close relationships with anyone. Since he appeared to be delusional, it was possible that his psychological structures would collapse in the face of imminent defeat. The most likely scenario was that he would commit suicide, although there was a possibility that he would order a henchman to perform euthanasia.

James A. Brussel

Between 1940 and 1956, a serial bomber terrorized New York City by planting bombs in public places including movie theaters, phone booths, Radio City Music Hall, Grand Central Terminal, and Pennsylvania Station. In 1956, the frustrated police requested a profile from Greenwich Village psychiatrist James A. Brussel, who was New York State's assistant commissioner of mental hygiene. Dr. Brussel studied photographs of the crime scenes and analyzed the so-called "mad bomber's" mail to the press. Soon he came up with a detailed description of the offender. In his profile, Dr. Brussel suggested that the unknown offender would be a heavy middle-aged man who was unmarried, but perhaps living with a sibling. Moreover, the offender would be a skilled mechanic from Connecticut, who was a Roman Catholic immigrant and, while having an obsessional love for his mother, would harbor a hatred for his father. Brussel noted that the offender had a personal vendetta against Consolidated Edison, the city's power company; the first bomb targeted its 67th Street headquarters. Dr. Brussel also mentioned to the police that, upon the offender's discovery, the "chances are he will be wearing a double-breasted suit. Buttoned."

From his profile, it was obvious to the police that the mysterious bomber would be a disgruntled current or unhappy former employee of Con Ed. The profile helped police to track down George Metesky in Waterbury, Connecticut; he had worked for Con Ed in the 1930s. He was arrested in January 1957 and confessed immediately. The police found Brussel's profile most accurate when they met the heavy, single, Catholic, and foreign-born Metesky. When the police told him to get dressed, he went to his bedroom and returned wearing a double-breasted suit, fully buttoned, just as Dr. Brussel had predicted. However, Malcolm Gladwell has written that offender profiling is not a science at all, but is couched in such ambiguous language that it can support almost any interpretation; and about Brussel says:

Brussel did not really understand the mind of the Mad Bomber. He seems to have understood only that, if you make a great number of predictions, the ones that were wrong will soon be forgotten, and the ones that turn out to be true will make you famous. The Hedunit is not a triumph of forensic analysis. It's a party trick.

Dr. Brussel assisted New York City police from 1957 to 1972 and profiled many crimes, including murder. Dr. Brussel also worked with other investigative agencies. Brussel's profile led the Boston Police to the apprehension of Albert DeSalvo, the notorious serial sex

275

murderer known as the Boston Strangler. The media dubbed Dr. Brussel as "Sherlock Holmes of the Couch".

Howard Teten

Howard D. Teten, a veteran police officer from California, joined the FBI in 1962. He was appointed as an instructor in applied criminology at the old National Police Academy in Washington, D.C. Teten was greatly interested in the application of offender profiling, and had included some of the ideas in his applied criminology course. He met Dr. Brussel and exchanged investigative ideas and psychological strategies in profiling crimes. Although Teten disagreed with Dr. Brussel's Freudian interpretations, he accepted other tenets of his investigative analysis.

In 1972 the FBI's Behavioral Science Unit at Quantico was formed, with Teten joining FBI Instructor Patrick J. Mullany's team. Teten and Mullany designed a method for analyzing unknown offenders in unsolved cases. The idea was to look at the behavioral manifestations at a crime scene for evidence of mental disorders and other personality traits, thus aiding the detectives' deductive reasoning. Their ideas on offender profiling were tested when a seven-year-old girl was abducted from a Rocky Mountains campsite in Montana in June 1973. The girl was abducted from a tent in the early hours; the offender overpowered her before she could alert her parents, who were sleeping nearby. When an intensive search for the missing child failed, the case was referred to the FBI.

Teten, Mullany and Col. Robert K. Ressler employed their criminal investigative analysis technique to track down the unknown offender. Their profile declared that the abductor was most likely a young, white, male, homicidal Peeping Tom; a sex killer who mutilates his victim after death, who sometimes takes body parts as souvenirs. Later, the profile led to the arrest of David Meirhofer, a local 23-year-old single man who was also a suspect in another murder case. The search of his house unearthed "souvenirs"—body parts taken from both victims. Meirhofer was the first serial killer to be caught with the aid of the FBI's new investigative technique, called offender profiling or criminal investigative analysis. A decade later, the technique became a more sophisticated and systematic profiling tool known as the Criminal Investigative Analysis Program (CIAP).

Richard Walter and Bob Keppel

In 1974, homicide detective Robert D. Keppel used new methods of psychological profiling to investigate notorious serial killers Ted Bundy and the Green River Killer. He combined his field expertise with criminal psychologist Richard Walter. As a psychologist in Michigan's notorious prison system, Walter had interviewed over two thousand murderers, sex-offenders and serial killers. Walter began to see common threads among offenders and was able to group all killings and sex crimes into four distinct "subtypes": power-assertive, power-reassurance, anger-retaliatory, and anger-excitation or sadism. He was the first to develop a matrix using suspect pre-crime, crime and post-crime behaviors as a tool for investigation. Walter later co-founded the

Vidocq society, an exclusive organization of forensic professionals who solve cold cases for law enforcement agencies, worldwide. Together, Keppel and Walter created the HITS (Hunter Integrated Telemetry System) database, which lists characteristics of violent crimes so that common threads can be investigated. They also published a leading scholarly article for the FBI and violent crime investigators all over the world: "Profiling Killers: A Revised Classification Model for Understanding Sexual Murder".

John Douglas and Robert Ressler

In 1978, after Howard Teten left the Behavioral Science Unit, John Douglas and Robert Ressler became pillars of offender profiling in the FBI. They spent much time studying convicted sex murderers and interviewing them, creating organized and disorganized typology, which is still in use today. Ressler was also responsible for the founding of the National Center for Analysis of Violent Crime (NCAVC) and at least partially responsible for the establishment of VICAP. Their studies provide more information on the behavioral patterns, traits and characteristics of criminals which can then be added to the offender profiling program.

David Canter

In 1986, police forces across the south of England were struggling to find the *Railway Rapist* who was then renamed the *Railway Killer* after murdering a victim for the first time. Dr. David Canter, a psychologist and criminologist then from Surrey University, was invited to compose British crime's first offender profile. When John Duffy was later arrested, charged and convicted, it turned out 13 of Canter's 17 proclamations about the perpetrator were accurate. Profiling became commonplace in large-scale police searches afterwards. David Canter came up with an equation that summarizes the principal research question in profiling: $A \Rightarrow C$. Canter defines 'A' as representing all actions that occur in a crime or that are related to a crime; 'C' represents the characteristics of the offender; '$\Rightarrow$' represents the scientific modeling that allows for inferences to be established regarding the characteristics from the actions.

Phases of profiling

According to Gregg O. McCrary, the basic premise is that behavior reflects personality. In a homicide case, for example, FBI profilers try to collect the personality of the offender through questions about his or her behavior at four phases:

1. **Antecedent:** What fantasy or plan, or both, did the murderer have in place before the act? What triggered the murderer to act some days and not others?
2. **Method and manner:** What type of victim or victims did the murderer select? What was the method and manner of murder: shooting, stabbing, strangulation or something else?
3. **Body disposal:** Did the murder and body disposal take place all at one scene, or multiple scenes?

4. **Post-offense behavior:** Is the murderer trying to inject himself into the investigation by reacting to media reports or contacting investigators?

A sexual crime is analyzed in much the same way (bearing in mind that homicide is sometimes a sexual crime), with the additional information that comes from a living victim. Professor David Canter is the pioneer of scientific offender profiling, developing the discipline of Investigative Psychology as a response to his dissatisfaction with the scientific bases for this activity. The IAIP of which Canter is President now seeks to set professional guidelines for practice and research in this area.

Another phase of criminal profiling (crime scene investigation) is case linkage. According to Brent E. Turvey, case linkage or linking analysis refers to the process of determining whether or not there are discrete connections between two or more previously unrelated cases through crime scene analysis. It involves establishing and comparing the physical evidence, victimology, crime scene characteristics, modus operandi (MO)-organized or disorganized typologies-, and signature behaviors between each of the cases under review. It has two purposes:

1. To assist law enforcement with the application of its finite resources by helping to establish where to apply investigative efforts
2. To assist the court in determining whether or not there is sufficient behavioral evidence to suggest a common scheme or plan in order to address

forensic issues, such as whether similar crimes may be tried together or whether other crimes may be brought in as evidence.

With respect to behavioral evidence, case linkage efforts have most typically hinged on three concepts:

1. MO, modus operandi
2. Signature
3. victimology

Problems

There are major problems with offender profiling that have been identified.

Incorrect information from profiling can lead to false positives or false negatives. Investigators may find a suspect who appears to fit an incorrect profile and ignore or stop investigating other leads. For example, Richard Jewell was wrongly investigated (and attacked in the media) following the Centennial Olympic Park bombing in Atlanta. This not only caused great distress to Jewell, but delayed identifying the true culprit, Eric Robert Rudolph. This was a false positive: the profile identified Jewell as the offender when in fact he was not. The opposite of the false positive is the false negative: the profile yields incorrect information which would cause investigators to ignore a suspect who is actually guilty. For example, in the Beltway sniper attacks, the offender profile indicated that the killer was probably a white male in his thirties from the DC area acting alone— in fact, the crimes were perpetrated by two black males, one of whom was 41 and the other 17 years old, from the west coast of the U.S.

The Peggy Hettrick murder case is controversial because it is the only documented case of an individual having been convicted due to a reversed engineered false profile and the erroneous testimony of the psychologist who developed the profile. In 1999, a jury convicted Timothy Masters of the 1987 killing of Peggy Hettrick. Masters spent over 9 years in a Colorado prison before his release on January 22, 2008. Timothy Masters was arrested and convicted of sexual murder based on the testimony of a forensic psychologist while the opinion of a Robert R. "Roy" Hazelwood, a retired FBI criminal investigative analyst was ignored. The forensic psychologist developed a psychological profile of a killer using narrative and drawings made by Masters to conclude that Masters' supposed fantasy was the motive and behavioral preparation for the sexual murder, regardless of the fact that the forensic psychologist knew that there was no direct or physical evidence linking Masters to the crime. The cautionary lesson in the Masters case is what happens when forensic psychologists advance opinions about criminal matters based on the extrapolation of academic research on psychological concepts involving sexual homicide cases and reject the opinions of professional criminal profilers who incorporate law enforcement analysis coupled with criminal evidentiary considerations into their work.

Some experts in criminal psychology such as Brent Turvey, as quoted by journalist Malcolm Gladwell in *The New Yorker* have questioned its scientific validity. Many profilers and FBI agents are not psychologists, and some researchers who looked at their work found methodological flaws.

Three psychologists from the Universities of Liverpool and Hull are questioning the basic presumption that you can draw conclusions about a person from a single instance of behaviour under such special circumstances. "The notion that particular configurations of demographic features can be predicted from an assessment of particular configurations of specific behaviors occurring in short-term, highly traumatic situations seems an overly ambitious and unlikely possibility. Thus, until such inferential processes can be reliably verified, such claims should be treated with great caution in investigations and should be entirely excluded from consideration in court."

Active profiling as allowed by the Department of Justice includes covert alteration of the environment to observe the responses of a suspect. This can be used to check whether the suspect's behavior fits the profile, but risks being labeled as police harassment or entrapment.

Popular use of the term *criminal profiler* has led to the proliferation of many self-described profilers offering their purported expert opinions on cable news shows in response to incidents capturing national attention in the United States. Such individuals usually have degrees in criminal justice or psychology but lack any law enforcement experience, or *vice versa*.

Chapter 4 – How To Protect Yourself on Social Media Sites

Cyber criminal activity is increasing at an exponential rate because it is the safest crime to commit. Cyber criminals know that committing cyber crimes below $50,000 are pretty much ignored by law enforcement. Law enforcement is in a big pickle here; it neither has the resources, budget, personnel or expertise to combat cyber crime and apprehend cyber criminals. Like it or not, each individual is left to protect themselves from the lurking cyber criminals and present the hardest target possible so they go off and attack a least prepared individual or business.

Areas of Personal EXPOSURE

- Credit Card Fraud
- Identity Theft
- Financial Scams
- Child Predation
- Computer Hijacking
- Malware
- Spyware
- Viruses
- Keystroke Logging
- Phishing
- User Account & Password Theft
- Cell Phone Spying
- Online Auction Fraud – Ebay, etc.
- And much more…

The above areas of personal exposure are the more prevalent forms of cyber crimes directed against individuals. It is by no means a complete list.

Be on the Lookout for…

Surfing the Web

One way that hackers get hold of you is when you surf the web. They put up enticing websites and as soon as you bring one up on your screen they are secretly downloading spyware onto your computer. Here are a few ways to protect yourself when web surfing:

Anonymizer: http://www.anonymizer.com/
Anonymouse:
http://www.anonymouse.org/anonwww.html
Identity Cloaker:
http://www.identitycloaker.com/?a_aid=neternatives
StartPage: https://www.startpage.com/
Tor Project: https://www.torproject.org/
Freenet Project: https://www.freenetproject.org/

You can also use various proxies to cloak your IP address:

Proxy Heaven: http://www.proxy-heaven.blogspot.com/
Proxy Services: http://www.proxyservices.com/
Your Private Proxy: http://www.yourprivateproxy.com/
HideMyAss: http://www.hidemyass.com/proxy-list/
MyPrivateProxy: http://www.myprivateproxy.net/

Cell Phone Spying

One of the easiest ways to become a victim of cyber-crime is by hacking into your cell phone and installing spyware. Today's Cell Phone spyware does not require that the hacker have possession of your phone. They simply call your cell phone number and whether it is answered or not, it takes all of about 30-seconds to marry your phone to the spyware.

Spyware of this type is readily available on the open market. Go here:
http://www.flexispy.com/?ref=1252800

Did you know that with the help of a simple, inexpensive device, anyone with access to your phone could read your private text messages (SMS), even if you have deleted them previously? This device can even recover contacts and a good number or previously dialed numbers. Go here:
http://www.brickhousesecurity.com/cellphone-spy-simcardreader.html

There is also a device that costs a whopping $20 that will tell you the cell phone number of any cell phone within 20-feet of the device. And "NO" we will not tell you where to get one or even what it is called.

The #1 Personal Intrusion is Cell Phone Spying

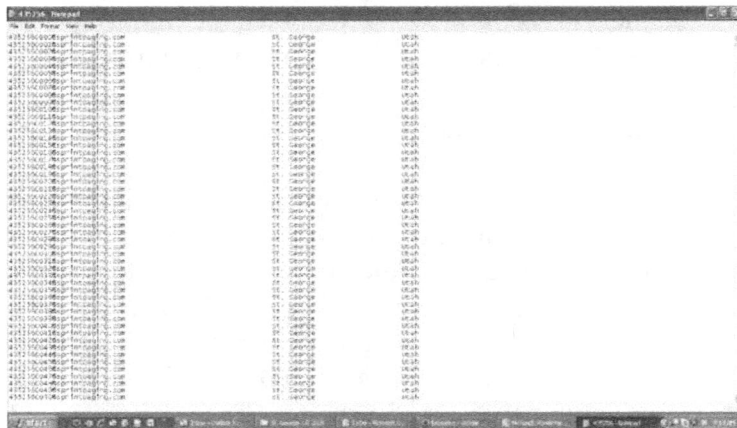

Where do hackers get your cell phone number?   See below and the best part is that it is FREE!

Cell Phone Spying Detection

Your Battery Temperature
One indicator of a possible phone tap is the temperature of your battery. Feel your cell phone if you haven't used it for a while. If it feels warm, this means your phone could be still in use, even if you are not on a call. Please note however that heat may be from overuse. Your battery being hot is only a potential sign if your phone has been powered down for a while.

Phone Not Staying Charged
Having to charge your cell phone more often than normal is another potential sign. If you haven't used it any more than usual, your phone could be in use when you aren't using it. When a cell phone is tapped it loses its battery life faster. A tapped cell phone is constantly recording conversations in the room, even when the phone appears to be idle. You can use an app like BatteryLife LX or Battery LED (iPhone) to monitor your phone's battery life and history over time.

[Note]: Cell phone batteries tend to lose the ability to stay charged over time. If you've had your phone for over a year, your battery may be going bad due to overuse and constant charging over time.

Delay in Shutting Down
When shutting down your phone, if you face issues such as a delay, the back light remaining lit for a time after being shut down, or refusal to shut off, your phone could be tapped. Always be aware of inexplicable activity on your phone. Since phones are made up of hardware and

software, however, this could also be caused due to a glitch in the system or some kind of internal problem as well.

More Strange Activity
While turned on, does your phone ever light up, shut down, power up, or install a program on its own? Strange activity could also be a sign of someone else controlling your device.

Note that this can also happen due to interference during the transmission of data.

Background Noise
When on a call, a tapped phone will often include background noises. Usually in the form of echoes, static, or clicking, these sounds can either be caused by interference, a bad connection, or someone else listening in. If you ever hear a pulsating static noise coming from your phone when you are not using it, however, you may have a problem.

Distortion
If you are using your cell phone in close proximity to other electronic devices, like a television, and the other devices become distorted, this could be a sign that additional hardware is installed in the cell phone. A lot of times this distortion is normal, but if it is happening while you're not on a call it could be something to watch for.

What Can You Do About This?
For tips on what you can do if you are ever in this situation, as well as a visual display of some of the signs

mentioned above, I invite you to watch this YouTube video entitled, "Is Your Cell Phone Bugged?":

http://www.youtube.com/watch?v=ujosfSkHFrQ

Email

Your email accounts can quite easily be hacked. There is software available on the open market that breaks usernames and passwords. Also, if your computer is hacked, most people leave sensitive information on their computer that can fall into a hacker's hands.

To protect your usernames and passwords use Roboform, which is 128-bit encrypted and virtually impossible to hack into:

http://www.roboform.com/php/pums/rfprepay.php?affid= ta556

You can also protect yourself by using a secure email service like Hushmail:

http://www.husmail.com

https://riseup.net/en

http://www.zoho.com/

https://www.hover.com/

Virtual Privacy Networks:

https://www.witopia.net/

https://www.privatvpn.se/en/

http://www.strongvpn.com

Identity Theft

Identity theft occurs when someone uses your personally identifying information, like your name, Social Security number, or credit card number, without your permission, to commit fraud or other crimes. The FTC estimates that as many as 9 million Americans have their identities stolen each year. In fact, you or someone you know may have experienced some form of identity theft.

The crime takes many forms. Identity thieves may rent an apartment, obtain a credit card, or establish a telephone account in your name. You may not find out about the theft until you review your credit report or a credit card statement and notice charges you didn't make—or until you're contacted by a debt collector.

Identity theft is serious. While some identity theft victims can resolve their problems quickly, others spend hundreds of dollars and many days repairing damage to their good name and credit record. Some consumers victimized by identity theft may lose out on job opportunities, or be denied loans for education, housing or cars because of negative information on their credit reports. In rare cases, they may even be arrested for crimes they did not commit.

How do thieves steal an identity?

Identity theft starts with the misuse of your personally identifying information such as your name and Social Security number, credit card numbers, or other financial account information. For identity thieves, this information is as good as gold. Skilled identity thieves may use a variety of methods to get hold of your information, including:

Dumpster Diving. They rummage through trash looking for bills or other paper with your personal information on it.

Skimming. They steal credit/debit card numbers by using a special storage device when processing your card.

Phishing. They pretend to be financial institutions or companies and send spam or pop-up messages to get you to reveal your personal information.

Changing Your Address. They divert your billing statements to another location by completing a change of address form.

Old-Fashioned Stealing. They steal wallets and purses; mail, including bank and credit card statements; pre-approved credit offers; and new checks or tax information. They steal personnel records, or bribe employees who have access.

Pretexting. They use false pretenses to obtain your personal information from financial institutions, telephone companies, and other sources.

What do thieves do with a stolen identity?

Once they have your personal information, identity thieves use it in a variety of ways.
Credit card fraud:

They may open new credit card accounts in your name. When they use the cards and don't pay the bills, the delinquent accounts appear on your credit report. They may change the billing address on your credit card so that you no longer receive bills, and then run up charges on your account. Because your bills are now sent to a different address, it may be some time before you realize there's a problem.

Phone or utilities fraud:
They may open a new phone or wireless account in your name, or run up charges on your existing account. They may use your name to get utility services like electricity, heating, or cable TV.

Bank/finance fraud:
They may create counterfeit checks using your name or account number. They may open a bank account in your name and write bad checks. They may clone your ATM or debit card and make electronic withdrawals your name, draining your accounts. They may take out a loan in your name.

Government documents fraud:
They may get a driver's license or official ID card issued in your name but with their picture. They may use your name and Social Security number to get government benefits. They may file a fraudulent tax return using your information.

Other fraud:
They may get a job using your Social Security number. They may rent a house or get medical services using your name. They may give your personal information to police during an arrest. If they don't show up for their court date, a warrant for arrest is issued in your name.

How can you find out if your identity was stolen?

The best way to find out is to monitor your accounts and bank statements each month, and check your credit report on a regular basis. If you check your credit report regularly, you may be able to limit the damage caused by identity theft.

Unfortunately, many consumers learn that their identity has been stolen after some damage has been done. You may find out when bill collection agencies contact you for overdue debts you never incurred. You may find out when you apply for a mortgage or car loan and learn that problems with your credit history are holding up the loan. You may find out when you get something in the mail about an apartment you never rented, a house you never bought, or a job you never held.

What should you do if your identity is stolen?

Filing a police report, checking your credit reports, notifying creditors, and disputing any unauthorized transactions are some of the steps you must take immediately to restore your good name.

Should you file a police report if your identity is stolen?

A police report that provides specific details of the identity theft is considered an Identity Theft Report, which entitles you to certain legal rights when it is provided to the three major credit reporting agencies or to companies where the thief misused your information. An Identity Theft Report can be used to permanently block fraudulent information that results from identity theft, such as accounts or addresses, from appearing on your credit report. It will also make sure these debts do not reappear on your credit reports. Identity Theft Reports can prevent a company from continuing to collect debts that result from identity theft, or selling them to others for collection. An Identity Theft Report is also needed to place an extended fraud alert on your credit report.

You may not need an Identity Theft Report if the thief made charges on an existing account and you have been able to work with the company to resolve the dispute. Where an identity thief has opened new accounts in your name, or where fraudulent charges have been reported to the consumer reporting agencies, you should obtain an Identity Theft Report so that you can take advantage of the protections you are entitled to.

In order for a police report to entitle you to the legal rights mentioned above, it must contain specific details about the identity theft. You should file an ID Theft Complaint with the FTC and bring your printed ID Theft Complaint with you to the police station when you file your police report. The printed ID Theft Complaint can be used to support your local police report to ensure that it includes the detail required.

A police report is also needed to get copies of the thief's application, as well as transaction information from companies that dealt with the thief.

Cyberstalking

Cyberstalking is the use of the Internet or other electronic means to stalk or harass an individual, a group of individuals, or an organization. It may include false accusations, monitoring, making threats, identity theft, damage to data or equipment, the solicitation of minors for sex, or gathering information in order to harass. The definition of "harassment" must meet the criterion that a reasonable person, in possession of the same information, would regard it as sufficient to cause another reasonable person distress. Cyberstalking is different from spatial or offline stalking. However, it sometimes leads to it, or is accompanied by it. When identifying cyberstalking and particularly when considering whether to report it to any kind of legal authority, the following features can be considered to characterize a true stalking situation: malice, premeditation, repetition, distress, obsession, vendetta, no legitimate purpose, personally directed, disregarded warnings to stop, harassment, and threats.

A number of key factors have been identified:

False accusations. Many cyberstalkers try to damage the reputation of their victim and turn other people against them. They post false information about them on websites. They may set up their own websites, blogs or user pages for this purpose. They post allegations about the victim to newsgroups, chat rooms or other sites that allow public contributions, such as Wikipedia or Amazon.com.

Attempts to gather information about the victim. Cyberstalkers may approach their victim's friends, family and work colleagues to obtain personal information. They may advertise for information on the Internet, or hire a private detective. They often will monitor the victim's online activities and attempt to trace their IP address in an effort to gather more information about their victims.

Encouraging others to harass the victim. Many cyberstalkers try to involve third parties in the harassment. They may claim the victim has harmed the stalker or his/her family in some way, or may post the victim's name and telephone number in order to encourage others to join the pursuit.

False victimization. The cyberstalker will claim that the victim is harassing him/her. Bocij writes that this phenomenon has been noted in a number of well-known cases.

Attacks on data and equipment. They may try to damage the victim's computer by sending viruses.

Ordering goods and services. They order items or subscribe to magazines in the victim's name. These often involve subscriptions to pornography or ordering sex toys then having them delivered to the victim's workplace.

Arranging to meet. Young people face a particularly high risk of having cyberstalkers try to set up meetings between them.

Types of Cyberstalkers

Of women
Harassment and stalking of women online is common, and can include rape threats and other threats of violence, as well as the posting of women's personal information. It is blamed for limiting victims' activities online or driving them offline entirely, thereby impeding their participation in online life and undermining their autonomy, dignity, identity and opportunities.

Of intimate partners
Cyberstalking of intimate partners is the online harassment of a current or former romantic partner. It is a form of domestic violence, and experts say its purpose is

to control the victim in order to encourage social isolation and create dependency. Harassers may send repeated insulting or threatening e-mails to their victims, monitor or disrupt their victims' e-mail use, and use the victim's account to send e-mails to others posing as the victim or to purchase goods or services the victim doesn't want. They may also use the internet to research and compile personal information about the victim, to use in order to harass her.

By anonymous online mobs
Web 2.0 technologies have enabled online groups of anonymous people to self-organize to target individuals with online defamation, threats of violence and technology-based attacks. These include publishing lies and doctored photographs, threats of rape and other violence, posting sensitive personal information about victims, e-mailing damaging statements about victims to their employers, and manipulating search engines to make damaging material about the victim more prominent. Victims are often women and minorities. They frequently respond by adopting pseudonyms or going offline entirely. A notable example of online mob harassment was the experience of American software developer and blogger Kathy Sierra. In 2007, a group of anonymous individuals attacked Sierra, threatening her with rape and strangulation, publishing her home address and Social Security number, and posting doctored photographs of her. Frightened, Sierra cancelled her speaking engagements and shut down her blog, writing "I will never feel the same. I will never be the same."

Experts attribute the destructive nature of anonymous online mobs to group dynamics, saying that groups with homogeneous views tend to become more extreme as members reinforce each other's beliefs, they fail to see themselves as individuals, so they lose a sense of personal responsibility for their destructive acts, they dehumanize their victims, which makes them more willing to behave destructively, and they become more aggressive when they believe they are supported by authority figures. Internet service providers and website owners are sometimes blamed for not speaking out against this type of harassment.

Corporate cyberstalking
Corporate cyberstalking is when a company harasses an individual online, or an individual or group of individuals harasses an organization. Motives for corporate cyberstalking are ideological, or include a desire for financial gain or revenge.

Perpetrators

Profile
Preliminary research has identified four types of cyberstalkers: the vindictive cyberstalkers noted for the ferocity of their attacks; the composed cyberstalker whose motive is to annoy; the intimate cyberstalker who attempts to form a relationship with the victim but turns on them if rebuffed; and collective cyberstalkers, groups with motive.
The general profile of the harasser is cold, with little or no respect for others. The stalker is a predator who can wait patiently until vulnerable victims appear, such as

women or children, or may enjoy pursuing a particular person, whether personally familiar to them or unknown. The harasser enjoys and demonstrates their power to pursue and psychologically damage the victim.

Behaviors
Cyberstalkers find their victims by using search engines, online forums, bulletin and discussion boards, chat rooms, and more recently, through social networking sites, such as MySpace, Facebook, Bebo, Friendster, Twitter, and Indymedia, a media outlet known for self-publishing.

They may engage in live chat harassment or flaming or they may send electronic viruses and unsolicited e-mails. Cyberstalkers may research individuals to feed their obsessions and curiosity. Conversely, the acts of cyberstalkers may become more intense, such as repeatedly instant messaging their targets. More commonly they will post defamatory or derogatory statements about their stalking target on web pages, message boards and in guest books designed to get a reaction or response from their victim, thereby initiating contact. In some cases, they have been known to create fake blogs in the name of the victim containing defamatory or pornographic content.

When prosecuted, many stalkers have unsuccessfully attempted to justify their behavior based on their use of public forums, as opposed to direct contact. Once they get a reaction from the victim, they will typically attempt to track or follow the victim's internet activity. Classic cyberstalking behavior includes the tracing of the victim's

303

IP address in an attempt to verify their home or place of employment.

Some cyberstalking situations do evolve into physical stalking, and a victim may experience abusive and excessive phone calls, vandalism, threatening or obscene mail, trespassing, and physical assault. Moreover, many physical stalkers will use cyberstalking as another method of harassing their victims.

Financial Fraud & Scams

Are There Anyways of Overcoming Cyber Fraud?

Internet is the fastest growing medium on earth that you would find these days and for everything it is the best solution that people consider looking into. Where it has all the benefits and advantages like communication, link building, advertisement, online movie downloads, online song downloads, emailing, instant messaging and searching out the concerns and issues there are plenty of things that internet has got wrong as well. There are multiple different kinds of internet scams and frauds that are out there that you have to be careful from. It is something that has been bothering individuals ever since internet was introduced and many times, simple things

304

could make you a victim when you won't even get to know of it.

The email scam is at the top of the internet scams and internet fake activities. People have had a routine of making money from different resources. You might have been through those false emails and messages that come into your inbox saying you won a lottery or you just made thousands of dollars from some resource which you don't even know of. These cyber fraud emails are often auto generated and are sent out to hundreds of people like you so they could enter their account information and even simple money transactions for those people to take benefits from. After paying the processing fee to the scammed email, the individuals would get no suitable response to it and they would rather be asked for the bank account information and different sort of things that could lead the scam artists to the big amount of money and funds.

You can stop cyber fraud by reporting them to the local police and even to the online websites that have an option to do so. Most of the time, people don't consider reporting such things because they are considered unimportant; this is the main reason why scammers are getting more confidence towards what they are doing. One of the other causes due to which this cyber fraud is spreading day by day is because people overlook the cyber laws and regulations that are made out by the websites and forums. People should get to know more about internet laws and what to do once they find out someone is not abiding by them in an effective manner. One should take out significant amount of time checking the emails and several other notifications online to see which ones are valid and which ones aren't.

Cyber fraud refers to any type of deliberate deception for unfair or unlawful gain that occurs online. The most common form is online credit card theft. Other common forms of monetary cyber fraud include nondelivery of paid products purchased through online auctions and nondelivery of merchandise or software bought online. Cyber fraud also refers to data break-ins, identity theft, and cyberbullying, all of which are seriously damaging.

Here's an example: A 20-year-old Facebook user posted: *"I eyed this girl on campus for months before I finally got the nerve to talk to her. I created an excuse to ask her a question and then started chatting her up. I must have given off the vibe that I was interested because right away, she dropped the bomb that she had a boyfriend. Bummed but not discouraged, I got my computer-savvy friend to hack into her boyfriend's Facebook account and change his relationship status to 'single.' The girl must have freaked out because the next thing I heard, they'd gotten into a huge fight and broken things off. A few days later, I asked her about her boyfriend, totally playing it off like I had no idea they were through. When she told me what had happened, I offered to take her out for coffee to get her mind off the breakup. My plan worked, because after our little date, she came back to my dorm room and we hooked up."*

Not all cyber fraud occurs through e-mail, but most of them do. Other methods are on the Internet itself. You may even get a letter through the post, because your postal address may have been captured by a spyware program or spam e-mail you replied to with your postal address included in the reply. Most scams exploit people's greediness. There is always promise of great returns on money you should invest in them. You can stay safe by following common sense and a few basic simple rules:

- Never send people money that contacted you by e-mail, or any other method in the Internet, period. Especially if you never heard of them before. What clear minded person will send money to a complete stranger?
- Never reply to, or click on any links in e-mails requesting personal, account or any kind of user information.
- Never reply to, or click on any links in e-mails from organizations you are not member of. Why will Amazon, PayPal, eBay, Barclays Bank, or any organization send you e-mail if you are not a member of them?
- Never reply to, or click on any links in lottery or competition e-mails, you never entered. How can you suddenly win a competition you never entered?

Another way to identify fraud is looking at the real URL the link in the e-mail points to. How do I do that? Well most of the popular e-mail clients have a status bar at the bottom of your screen. If you hover with your mouse cursor above the link, the URL (Uniform Resource Locator, in other words, the exact web address it points to) will appear in the status bar. These links should point to the main domain of the company.

For instance the links in e-mail from PayPal should start with www.paypal.com, nothing else. If it starts with something like www.pay-pal.com, www.pay.pal.com, www.paypal_.com, www.paypalsecure.com or any variation of the real domain, then it's fraudulent, even if it points to a secure server (These links start with https:// and not the standard http://).

Any variation of the real domain points to a different server, not owned by PayPal, where you can get infected by viruses, spyware, adware, or become victim of a hacking attempt.

What is the #1 Internet Scam today?

U.S. Colleges and Universities Most Favored Target for Phishing

Phishing attacks against colleges and universities are focused on stealing the login credentials that students use to access all their personal university-related information and email; credentials that usually consist of students' usernames and passwords. Why phishers are seeking out students' information?

1. Young naïve girls ripe for cyberstalking and;
2. Application for financial aid or bogus student loans, as demonstrated by a recent case in Arizona.

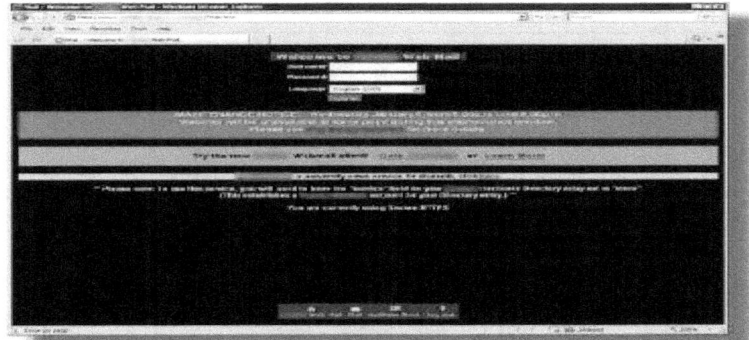

Phishing attack masquerading as a University's Webmail portal

Phishing attack disguised as a University's login page

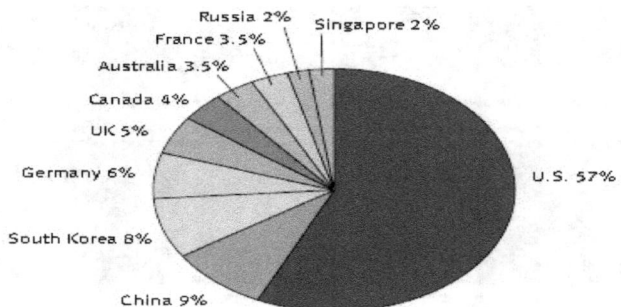

Top Ten Countries Hosting Phishing Attacks

Computer Hijacking

Computer Hijacking is a crime where the criminal takes over your computer and you are unable to control anything that is being done to your computer. This is a federal offence and the criminal will be jailed if caught.

How to protect against computer hijacking and against theft of your personal data (with potential to be used in Identity Theft).

Hijacking can only happen when hijacker's software finds its way to your computer. Identity theft comes with unauthorized access to your information.

So the best way to protect is:

Don't let them in!

Keep out software that you do not trust, *such as*:
- Any suspicious e-mail attachments

- Files downloaded from strange places
- ActiveX and Plugins from untrusted sites
- Use Spyware

To achieve this you need
- Several building blocks to be in place:
- Patch your browsers.
- Antivirus product.
- Anti spyware product.
- Personal firewall

You should look after your protection software:

- Keep them up-to-date.
- Check them regularly (for example - weekly) that automatic update is really working.
- Configure your software (like antivirus) to scan your computer daily (at night or at lunch time)

Keep software on your computers patched. Attackers would not be able to exploit known vulnerabilities and execute their programs through security holes.

To achieve that –

- Keep and maintain list of software you have installed
- Check for updates for each package regularly. Switch ON automatic checking for updates whenever it is possible.
- Note: Do you use MS Office? When did you check for MS Office update last time? Burn critical updates, Service Packs, Product Releases etc. on the two blank CDs and store one on site and one off site. *List of*

what I think is critical for the current versions of Windows OS could be found on this site soon.

Keep you data safe and available for restore in case that something does happen.

You will need your important information be available ASAP.

To achieve this -

- Identify data that should be preserved
- Keep your business related data files (such as drawings,
  plans, documents, presentations, program, schedules, lists of customers) in well identified places on your hard drive (or server)
- Check where is your e-mail program keeps your mail box and address book.
- Back up that data regularly.
- Check that backed up data can be restored correctly and actually used. Do it regularly
- Store back up media outside your main office.

This would help as part of any disaster. Power failure could destroy your hard drives. Thieves could steal your computers. You would need your data to keep business running.

So to make a conclusion:

Create the list what should be done and how often. Check   that   it   is   achievable

Make schedule out of it. Put it in your dairy (electronic or paper). Follow it
Review it when necessary.

Keystroke Logging - Phishing

Keystroke logging (often called **keylogging**) is the action of tracking (or logging) the keys struck on a keyboard, typically in a covert manner so that the person using the keyboard is unaware that their actions are being monitored. There are numerous keylogging methods, ranging from hardware and software-based approaches to electromagnetic and acoustic analysis.

Software-based keyloggers
A logfile from a software-based keylogger
A control window from a software-based keylogger
These are software programs designed to work on the target computer's operating system. From a technical perspective there are five categories:

Hypervisor-based: The keylogger can theoretically reside in a malware hypervisor running underneath the operating system, which remains untouched. It effectively becomes a virtual machine. Blue Pill is a conceptual example.

Kernel-based: This method is difficult both to write and to combat. Such keyloggers reside at the kernel level and are thus difficult to detect, especially for user-mode applications. They are frequently implemented as rootkits that subvert the operating system kernel and gain unauthorized access to the hardware, making them very powerful. A keylogger using this method can act as a keyboard device driver for example, and thus gain access to any information typed on the keyboard as it goes to the operating system.

API-based: These keyloggers hook keyboard APIs; the operating system then notifies the keylogger each time a key is pressed and the keylogger simply records it. Windows APIs such as GetAsyncKeyState, GetForegroundWindow, etc. are used to poll the state of the keyboard or to subscribe to keyboard events. These types of keyloggers are the easiest to write, but where constant polling of each key is required, they can cause a noticeable increase in CPU usage, and can also miss the occasional key. A more recent example simply polls the BIOS for pre-boot authentication PINs that have not been cleared from memory.

Form grabbing based: Form grabbing-based keyloggers log web form submissions by recording the web browsing onsubmit event functions. This records form data before it is passed over the Internet and bypasses HTTPS encryption.

Memory injection based: Memory Injection (MITB)-based keyloggers alter memory tables associated with the browser and other system functions to perform their logging functions. By patching the memory tables or injecting directly into memory, this technique can be used by malware authors who are looking to bypass Windows UAC (User Account Control). The Zeus and Spyeye Trojans use this method exclusively.

314

Packet analyzers: This involves capturing network traffic associated with HTTP POST events to retrieve unencrypted passwords.

Remote access software keyloggers - These are local software keyloggers with an added feature that allows access to the locally recorded data from a remote location. Remote communication may be achieved using one of these methods:

- Data is uploaded to a website, database or an FTP server.
- Data is periodically emailed to a pre-defined email address.
- Data is wirelessly transmitted by means of an attached hardware system.

The software enables a remote login to the local machine from the Internet or the local network, for data logs stored on the target machine to be accessed.

Used by police - In 2000, the FBI used a keystroke logger to obtain the PGP passphrase of Nicodemo Scarfo, Jr., son of mob boss Nicodemo Scarfo. Also in 2000, the FBI lured two suspected Russian cyber criminals to the US in an elaborate ruse, and captured their usernames and passwords with a keylogger that was covertly installed on a machine that they used to access their computers in Russia. The FBI then used these credentials to hack into the suspects' computers in Russia in order to obtain evidence to prosecute them.

Countermeasures - The effectiveness of countermeasures varies, because keyloggers use a variety of techniques to capture data and the countermeasure needs to be effective against the particular data capture technique. For example, an on-screen keyboard will be effective against hardware keyloggers, transparency will defeat some screenloggers - but not all - and an anti-spyware application that can only disable hook-based keyloggers will be ineffective against kernel-based keyloggers.

Also, keylogger software authors may be able to update the code to adapt to countermeasures that may have proven to be effective against them.

Anti keyloggers - An anti keylogger is a piece of software specifically designed to detect keyloggers on your computer, typically comparing all files in your computer against a database of keyloggers looking for similarities which might signal the presence of a hidden keylogger. As anti keyloggers have been designed specifically to detect keyloggers, they have the potential to be more effective than conventional antivirus software; some antivirus software do not consider certain keyloggers a virus, as under some circumstances a keylogger can be considered a legitimate piece of software.

User Account – Password Theft

Use a password management program, which stores all of my passwords safely under one master password.

The key is to make sure you have a strong master password for your password management program to protect your list of passwords. You'll want to create strong passwords for each site that you log into as well.

A strong password must have at least 8 characters (the longer the better), with a mixture of upper and lower-case letters, numbers and, if the site or service allows, special characters, such as "!," "#" and "?." It should be something you can remember easily. A long sentence works well when you take the first letter of each word and then substitute the vowels for numbers or symbols.

For example: The quick brown fox jumped inside the orange box and slept = Tqbfj1t0b&s

Once you've created your master password, you can set up your password manager. It stores your passwords and user names in an encrypted database, enabling you to quickly access them. Once you have your password manager running, it fills in your user ID and password for you.

The free Mozilla Firefox Web browser for PCs and Macs has a built-in password manager, but you need to make sure you create a master password to protect your list. Other browsers — Internet Explorer, Safari and Chrome — can remember passwords for you, but they do not have a manager or master password to protect your passwords, so it's best to use a dedicated program.

For stand-alone password managers, one of the best is RoboForm Everywhere, which works with Macs and PCs, as well as iPhones and Android phones. The program can auto-fill just about any online form, including email, name, phone number and credit card information.

http://www.roboform.com/php/pums/rfprepay.php?affid=ta556

And for Macs (and PCs), check out 1Password ($49.95 at agilewebsolutions.com). The software saves passwords, credit card numbers, account registration information, just about anything you can think of, and auto-fills it all across most browsers on a Mac, including Safari, Firefox and Camino.

There's also an app for iPhone and iPad ($9.99 in iTunes) that will sync with your desktop and stop you from having to peck out your passwords on that tiny touchscreen keyboard.

Hard Drive & Disc Encryption
Hacking your hard drive and other data storage devices can be preventing by using a free disc encryption program called TrueCrypt:

http://www.truecrypt.org/docs/

TrueCrypt encrypts everything on your hard drive and all your personal information and is virtually impossible to bust into and hack.

Here are a few more encryption providers:

http://www.endoacustica.com/index_en.htm
http://www.hotspotshield.com/

Miscellaneous Protection

The Best Firewall: http://www.comodo.com/

Stop Unwanted Mail: https://www.catalogchoice.org/

Secure Mailing Address: http://www.earthclassmail.com/

Secure VOIP Phone: http://zfoneproject.com/

Secure Chat Room: https://crypto.cat/

You can review chat room logs using this:
http://www.pimall.com/nais/chatstick.html#

You can detect PORN on any computer instantly:

http://www.pimall.com/nais/porndetectionstick.html#

Identify weaknesses and vulnerabilities in your personal computer:

http://www.eeye.com/products/retina/retina-network-scanner

Secure Search Engine

http://duckduckgo.com/

Privacy Apps for your browser

http://news.ghostery.com/
http://abine.com/dntdetail.php

I Have a Special Gift for My Readers

I appreciate my readers for without them I am just another author attempting to make a difference. If my book has made a favorable impression please leave me an honest review.   Thank you in advance for you participation.

My readers and I have in common a passion for the written word as well as the desire to learn and grow from books.

My special offer to you is a massive ebook library that I have compiled over the years. It contains hundreds of fiction and non-fiction ebooks in Adobe Acrobat PDF format as well as the Greek classics and old literary classics too.

In fact, this library is so massive to completely download the entire library will require over 5 GBs open on your desktop.

Use the link below and scan all of the ebooks in the library. You can select the ebooks you want individually or download the entire library.

The link below does not expire after a given time period so you are free to return for more books rather than clog your desktop. And feel free to give the link to your friends who enjoy reading too.

I thank you for reading my book and hope if you are pleased that you will leave me an honest review so that I can improve my work and or write books that appeal to your interests.

Okay, here is the link…

http://tinyurl.com/special-readers-promo

PS: If you wish to reach me personally for any reason you may simply write to mailto:support@epubwealth.com.

I answer all of my emails so rest assured I will respond.

Meet the Author

Dr. Harry Jay is Director of Research for AppliedMindSciences.com, a mental health and mind research group of Applied Web Info, and is the author of over 100 books and research papers as a behavioral scientist.

In his 32-year career, Dr. Harry Jay has contributed many new mental health treatment treatments and protocols using some of the new advances he has discovered in Energy Psychology.

He specializes in addictions of all kinds, sexual abuse, child predation and gender relationships.

He is also a board member to ePubWealth.com and serves on the science committee assisting non-fiction science writers in book publishing and promotion.

As a leading behavioral scientist, he provides profiling services to the company's ForensicsNation.com unit as well as criminal psychology research to aid in identifying and apprehending child predators and cyber-criminals of all kinds.

He resides in Southern Utah and enjoys the outdoors, fishing and photography.

Visit some of his websites

http://www.AddMeInNow.com
http://www.AppliedMindSciences.com
http://www.BookbuilderPLUS.com
http://www.BookJumping.com
http://www.EmailNations.com
http://www.EmbarrassingProblemsFix.com
http://www.ePubWealth.com
http://www.ForensicsNation.com
http://www.ForensicsNationStore.com
http://www.FreebiesNation.com
http://www.HealthFitnessWellnessNation.com
http://www.Neternatives.com
http://www.PrivacyNations.com
http://www.RetireWithoutMoney.org
http://www.SurvivalNations.com
http://www.TheBentonKitchen.com
http://www.Theolegions.org
http://www.VideoBookbuilder.com

Some Other Books You May Enjoy From ePubWealth.com, LLC Library Catalog

EPW Library Catalog Online
http://www.epubwealth.com/wp-content/uploads/2013/07/Leland-benton-private-turbo.pdf

EPW Library Catalog Download
http://www.filefactory.com/f/562ef3ea1a054f0a

www.ingramcontent.com/pod-product-compliance
Lightning Source LLC
Chambersburg PA
CBHW051759170526
45167CB00005B/1807